What physicians and colleagues are saying

This book offers valuable tips for new representatives starting out as well as seasoned reps. An excellent companion, the tips contained in this book will help representatives get a jump start in their careers. Quite often, training programs focus on the product and how to sell it. This book provides guidelines to follow in areas (from e-mail essentials to ordering wine) that many programs neglect, yet are essential in building business and optimizing success.

    – Juli Fyfe, CTDP, Manager, Sales Force Development, Bayer

This book on relationship-building is very practical and provides value for pharmaceutical professionals at all levels, from people new to the industry, to more experienced professionals. There is something in this book for all of us.

    – Chantale Fortin Sanofi-Synthelabo
Quebec Regional Manager, Specialty Sales Force

I see *Prescription for Success* as a "Training Tool for Success." It clearly demonstrates the necessity of focusing on communication, relationship building, and understanding and meeting the health care professionals' needs vs. the representatives' agendas. This book is full of pearls of wisdom and is a terrific gem for both new and experienced pharmaceutical representatives.

    – Gayle Waylett, R.D.N., MPH Western Regional Sales Manager
Novartis Nutrition Corporation

Excellent reminder of the simple principles of selling. This book is a "must read" for new as well as experienced pharmaceutical representatives. It will help you focus on the important elements of selling.

– **Gilles Lachance, General Manger, CCPE**

Cultural awareness and sensitivity will open many doors, and build lasting relationships that are the basis of our success in selling to any physician. The chapter "Across Cultures" takes you through the journey in simple, easy to understand examples. It provides tremendous insights on cultural differences around the world and tells you how to deal with them. This book will help you achieve your goals of effective selling to the foreign-born physician.

– **Francisco Rozo MD, Director**
Global Marketing Training
Novartis Oncology.

Prescription for Success is relevant, practical and immediately applicable. It should prove invaluable for both newly hired and experienced sales professionals in the pharma/biotech industries. It provides a solid foundation for sales professionals, covering many topics not previously included in traditional industry training.

– **Randy Lowe, Former Director**
Sales Training & Development
Roche Canada

This book contains astute observations that any sales representative could benefit from in building relationships with physicians.

– **Debra Finestone, MD**

Rapport is one of the most important keys to success in our industry, because people buy from people they like. Once rapport is established, you need to leverage it into a business opportunity. This is what the most successful representatives do. This book will help you do this.

– **Marc Buxbaum**
Director of Sales Training
Salix Pharmaceuticals Inc.

Anyone can buy a relationship with entertainment and incentives. To make a difference and be recognized as a partner, learn to add value to your relationships. This book offers you suggestions on how to achieve that goal!

– **Bob Chester**
Professional Education Manager
Aventis

This book is a very useful resource, most especially for the representative new to the industry. However, I myself picked up some useful tips throughout the book.

– **Jeff Burtis**
Manager, Sales Training & Development
Solvay Pharma

Through a step-by-step approach this book builds our awareness and helps to develop a successful relationship with health-care professionals.

– Wayne Hartman, Sales Training and Development
Wyeth Canada

Hélène Meloche and Christie Sterns have brought the interaction of their seminars into a practical and useable resource for pharmaceutical sales representatives. *Prescription for Success* provides an interactive exchange between the reader and the authors. A "must read" for representatives eager to open and keep open the doors to their physician's offices.

– Kimberly A. Farrell, President
Unlimited Performance Training, Inc.

There is a natural tendency for pharmaceutical sales professionals to rely too heavily on product information rather than relationships, when it's the latter that spells the difference between success and failure. *Prescription for Success* should be required reading for everyone in the pharmaceutical business.

– Barry Siskind
International Training and Management Company

This "easy-read" is packed full of useful tips – both professionally and personally. Although written for pharmaceutical professionals, the information provided would be of use to any professional who is in the service industry.

– Robin Preece
School Principal, Edmonton Public Schools

There is a ton of practical information that anyone can use right away! Just follow the instructions in this book. It covers everything in simple and easy-to-follow steps. This book will have value for me in establishing new clients and strengthening my relationships with my current clients.

> – Rosemary Frei, President
> Frei & Associates Communications

This book is extremely valuable as it reinforces the skills necessary to communicate with others in building relationships, and gives you comprehensive summaries on topics such as business etiquette and how to choose the right wine for dinner.

> – Ross Vaccari, Prelude

The one-minute lessons in *Prescription for Success* give good, quick information, with valuable industry workplace examples. The content would be applicable to recent university graduates, but also to experienced employees who may be new to the pharmaceutical industry, or to anyone who wants to confirm that they are on the right tract.

> – Donna Poag. Instructional Design Consultant
> Poag & Associates Inc.

Capturing airtime: you've got 5 minutes. This book shows you how to make each one count.

> – Diane Bussandri, Managing Partner
> Knightsbridge Bussandri Macdonald

We all know that sustainable long-term relationships are based on credibility and service. It is a road well traveled and yet never really clearly defined. What appears "intuitive" to seasoned pharmaceutical professionals actually takes years of learning, based on costly mistakes. Experience and buddy-system learning have been the only way to really get "it"!

Prescription for Success, actually puts "it" on paper, in a book full of all those hidden gems. It will identify for some and verify for others, this complex set of skills, so very essential to pharmaceutical sales.

Rather than a "prescription," this should be available "OTC"!

– Lesley Scharf, BASc, RD
Head of Medical Education/Communication
Nestlé Nutrition

An experienced industry person might say that a lot of the ideas in this text are very much "common sense," yet common sense is not all that common! For both new and experienced industry personnel, this books serves as a series of best practices and valuable tips to help you navigate through what can be one of the most challenging yet rewarding careers I can think of. Every great journey requires a map to guide you, not only for those who haven't taken the journey before, but also for those of us who could use some gentle reminders of the best roads to take.

– John Brenton
Sales & Marketing Training Manager
Amgen Canada Inc.

Prescription *for Success*

Building Relationships for the Pharmaceutical and Biotech Industries

Hélène Meloche
and
Christie Sterns

with
Lynda Goldman

Helix Publishing

Helix Publishing
Text copyright © 2004

ATTENTION: Quantity discounts and customized versions of the book are available for bulk purchases.

Contact:

Lynda Goldman
2216 Mediterranean St.
Montreal, Quebec
Canada H4R 3B1

Tel: (514) 336-4339
Fax: (514) 336-9805
Toll-free: 1-877-462-4384
E-mail: Lynda@Prescription4success.com
www.Prescription4success.com

National Library of Canada Cataloguing in Publication

Meloche, Hélène, date-

   Prescription for success: building relationships for
the pharmaceutical and biotech industries / Hélène Meloche,
Christie Sterns, Lynda Goldman; edited by Sandra Thibaudeau.

ISBN 0-9694996-9-8

   I. Selling--Drugs. I. Sterns, Christie, date- II. Goldman,
Lynda, date-   IV. Title.

HF5439.D75M44 2003   615'.1'0688   C2003-905795-X

Editing: Tara Berish and Sandra Thibaudeau
Cover design: Grant Loewen, C & G Graphics

Printed and bound in Canada

2nd printing

Thanks to our contributing authors:

Diane Bussandri, Managing Partner, Knightsbridge Bussandri Macdonald, *Emotional Intelligence*

Frema Engel, Engel & Associés, *Resolving Conflict*

Vic Harradine, *Ordering Wine*

Janet MacPhee, Compass Coaching, *Listening and Questioning*

Barry Siskind, International Training and Management Company, *Exhibits and Conventions*

Acknowledgements and appreciation

We would like to acknowledge everyone who gave us input, suggestions and quotes. Your contributions and feedback were invaluable in shaping this book. Our gratitude and thanks go to:

Sophie Archambault, Dr. Alfred Balbul, Cindy Bernstein, Michel Brasseur, John Brenton, Michael E. Brown, Jeff Burtis, Diane Bussandri, Marc Buxbaum, Denis Campeau, Dr. Sophie Centazzo, Bob Chester, Julie Drewitt, Dr. M. Tray Dunaway, Frema Engel, Kimberly A. Farrell, Dr. Debra Finestone, Chantale Fortin, Rosemary Frei, Juli Fyfe, Cathy Good, Vic Harradine, Linda Hooper, Dr. Dyan Kimia, Gilles Lachance, Teri Laflamme, Randy Lowe, Janet McPhee, Nancy Smith Meloche, Nas Merali, Donna Poag, Robin Preece, Karen Pritchard, Jean Proulx, Raynald Riverin, Dr. Francisco Rozo, Leon Sergent, Barry Siskind, Ross Vaccari, Vicky Vilagos, Gayle Waylett

Special thanks to Christian R. Meloche for solving our computer challenges.

Our appreciation to Dr. Andy Farah for your suggestions and feedback, and for writing the foreword to this book.

To René, who always supported my dreams, and to Christian, Nancy and Audrey, and Yannick and Isabelle - the prides of my life.

To the loves of my life - John, Rebecca and Danielle.

CONTENTS

Contents

Contents

Prescription for Success is a practical source for all pharmaceutical professionals. Hélène, Christie and Lynda take a unique approach to building relationships by breaking down piece by piece, the elements of success in this competitive industry. This book is a resource guide to be referred to throughout your career.

— **Mari-Lynn Wells**
Medical Education Manager
Janssen-Ortho Inc.

Thank you very much for your book *Prescription for Success*. I just returned last night from Europe and read the book on the flight. It was a great re-fresher even for an old-timer like myself and I believe I picked up some new nuggets!

— **Rod Wilson, President and COO**
SYN-X Pharma Inc.

Introduction

Dear Pharmaceutical Colleague,

Congratulations on having a job in the pharmaceutical or biotech industry. You have been chosen to work in a field where you can have a positive influence on people's health.

You are an expert in your products and the medical specialty where your products are sold. When you represent your company, you are your company to that customer or to the public.

Unlike other industries where the goal is getting customers to sign on the bottom line, in the pharmaceutical industry you must take on a consultative approach. You have the opportunity to become an educator and a partner to physicians, providing information that helps them make the best choices for their patients.

Physicians put the health of patients, as well as their reputations, on the line. For physicians to prescribe your products, they must first feel confident working with you. To inspire trust and confidence, you must first build relationships.

Dr. Andy Farah, author of *The Doctor as Customer* and *The Ultimate Guide for Pharmaceutical Reps*, says, "Take time to really learn about your customers, their personal likes, their families, and of course learn all you can about their practices. This will lay the groundwork for relationship-based selling. Develop relationships so that when you walk in you are greeted as a friend. Eventually you'll become a partner in the business of patient care." We are honored that Dr. Farah took time from his busy practice to write the foreword to this book.

In the pharmaceutical and biotech industries, product knowledge is critical. Building relationships with the people you work with is equally critical. This book shows you how.

How this book can help you:

Prescription for Success focuses on the unique needs of pharmaceutical and biotech industry employees. It is the culmination of many years of experience in the pharmaceutical industry. Since 1985, Hélène Meloche and Christie Sterns have been training and coaching thousands of pharmaceutical industry employees in selling and communication skills. This book provides practical tips and valuable relationship-building lessons that they have developed in their training programs.

```
A D V
T I P
```
If you have been in the industry for several years, this book is for you as well. Look for the Advanced Tip sections for information that even the most seasoned representative can use. From dealing with the challenges of selling to doctors after the relationship becomes too friendly, or adapting your selling techniques to doctors from different cultures, you'll find many "best practice" tips from experienced, successful sales representatives.

Each chapter ends with quotes from physicians or pharmaceutical managers, who give their thoughts on the best ways to build relationships in the pharmaceutical and biotech industries.

How to use this book:

Prescription for Success is organized into powerful one-minute lessons. Each page has a separate idea within a thematic chapter. You can read the book from beginning to end, but feel free to skip around to the sections that are most relevant to you. The key ideas are summed up in *connection capsules* at the end of each chapter, and at the back of the book as well. You will also find a resource section with suggestions for further reading.

Here are some symbols and acronyms used in the book:

CME: Continuing Medical Education

CHE: Continuing Health Education

(These terms are used synonymously)

SMART Goals: Specific, Measurable, Achievable, Relevant and Time-limited

WII-FM: What's In It For Me?

Connection capsules: Encapsulate key ideas from the book

ADV
TIP

Expert tips for seasoned sales representatives

Use the tools in this book to help you build relationships that matter. Mixed with your own unique personality and genuine desire to reach your goals, you'll have your own "prescription for success."

You are lucky to have a job that makes a difference in people's lives. Best wishes for your continued success.

Hélène Meloche, Christie Sterns & Lynda Goldman

Foreword from Dr. Andy Farah

Each year since 1997 I have surveyed my physician colleagues to explore exactly where we get the information that we use to help our patients. Each year, your role as educators gains ground; more of us rely on you and your product details than any other source – such as Internet searches or scientific journals – for the facts we need.

With this role comes an awesome responsibility. But before you can help the thousands of patients that will be impacted, you need to gain access, engage in a discussion of real quality and value to that customer, and above all, be persuasive. Success in all these steps will depend on your relationship with each of the health care providers you detail.

On the day I met Lynda Goldman, I had been on hospital rounds only an hour before. It was a typical busy Monday on a psychiatric ward. A new patient was eager to see me because he believed that he was the Messiah, and needed to be discharged immediately. He had to get to a TV station as quickly as possible to share his message of hope. I asked the nurse who provided these details if he said he was "Christ the Messiah." She replied, "No, he says he's Herman the Messiah, which is odd, because his name is Anthony."

I hated to keep this Messiah waiting, but I noticed a sales representative at the nurses' station that I needed to see. This representative and I have a terrific relationship, and I usually drop whatever I am doing to see her. That day was no exception, particularly since I needed her input on potential drug interactions before I prescribed medication for the Messiah in room 514. This representative really is part of my treatment team – and I kept the Messiah waiting because of my relationship with Jana. But more to the point, the patient was best served by my visit and discussions with Jana.

You want all of your customers to see you in exactly this way: their time spent with you *is* how they put the patient first. That's why you have this book. But this book is unlike most of the sales books you have encountered. Many writers tell you to "build a relationship with customers," but don't tell you how. That's like telling depressed patients to feel better without giving them antidepressants and cognitive therapy.

Hélène Meloche, Christie Sterns and Lynda Goldman actually give you the tools you need to build relationships so you achieve success. No detail is left out of these pages, from advice on how much eye contact is appropriate in the sales setting, to making your speaker programs a huge success. The authors are not afraid to tackle the tough issues either, such as dealing with conflict in the relationship and turning it into a real opportunity to advance, or adjusting your details according to cultural differences among your customers. Their "connection capsules" will serve as your survival guide in the field.

As physician educators and fellow professionals, you have the potential to impact the lives of thousands of people you may never meet. It all hinges on the relationships you develop with your customers. The tools are here. Read on, and best of luck!

— Andy Farah, MD
Author of *The Doctor as Customer*,
The Ultimate Guide for Pharmaceutical Reps

Chapter I

RELATIONSHIP BUILDING BLOCKS

Establishing bonds and building connections

> The deepest principle in human nature is the craving to be appreciated.
>
> – William James

1. How to get people to want to work with you and buy from you

Why would anyone want to buy from you, or work with you? What do you bring to the table? In today's competitive pharmaceutical industry, product knowledge is critical. Knowing your job well, and doing it competently are vital. But if you fail to build relationships, you may soon find that people don't buy your products, or choose to work with you. If that happens, no amount of intelligence or hard work can save your job.

The simple truth is that it's in our nature to connect with people, and to build affiliations. We feel good about relating to others. But often things such as ego, jealousy, fear of rejection, and fear of appearing vulnerable get in the way. They keep us from making connections and building valuable relationships.

At the core of any productive and enjoyable relationship is a feeling of trust and respect. Relating well with customers and colleagues is crucial to your career success.

2. How do you want to be perceived?

Business professionals in a variety of fields were asked: "How do you want to be perceived in your work?" Their answers included: competent, confident, trustworthy, reliable, intelligent, approachable, smart, and capable. Not a single person said, "I want to confuse people so they aren't sure if they can trust me."

If you work with health care professionals, you know that these people work on tight schedules in hectic environments. You have to be able to work within their time constraints, and with gate-keepers such as receptionists who are responsible for protecting and managing their bosses' time.

A busy physician may see several industry employees in a week, or even in a single day. Demonstrating trustworthiness and professionalism are vital to starting and sustaining relationships that will lead to your success.

In *The Ultimate Guide for Pharmaceutical Reps,* Dr. Andy Farah describes a situation where he and his partner hurried through rounds because a representative scheduled lunch for their office, and twice the representative failed to show up. As Dr. Farah says, "All we really sell in medicine is our time. If you book some, please come!"

3. How to establish your credibility

Chantal meets with Dr. Ranger and promises to send her a new clinical study. Chantal's promise slips her mind, and she never sends the reprint. Chantal's slip-up cost her more than one sale. It cost her the chance to establish credibility with Dr. Ranger.

When we don't show up, or do what we say we will do, we lose credibility. In *The Doctor as Customer,* Dr. Andy Farah writes, "With the explosion of medical information, the real key today is not having all the answers, but knowing where to find them. You are one of the most valuable resources we have, so respect that privilege and strive for accuracy when discussing your drug and even when discussing the competition. If you 'fudge the facts', or provide bad information, you lose credibility. And let's face it, when you're in the business of providing information to doctors, what you are really selling is your credibility."

There are times when we make promises and don't deliver. Perhaps we are feeling helpful and generous at the moment, and we haven't thought about the feasibility of what we agreed to do. When we fail to keep our word, clients and colleagues won't believe us, or believe in us.

 We make a real impact when we under-promise and over-deliver.

4. How to develop relationships based on trust

Our society is programmed not to trust. We don't trust business or institutions. We don't trust processes. We trust people. People buy from another person, not from a company. We may associate the trusted person with their company, but we are still trusting a person, and not giving blanket trust to an institution.

Brand name recognition may get your company's name on a short list, but only the person representing the company can keep it there. In order to trust someone, we have to perceive that they understand our needs. Organizations can't do that, only people can.

People often say, "It's not personal, it's business." But business is personal. It's based on relationships. Trust develops over time, through gradual give and take. If I'm the customer, I will trust you if I feel that you're in this for the long haul, not the short term gain. I need to know that I can depend on you to do your part, and that our relationship is built on mutual values and goals.

Trusting relationships are based on mutual interest. In the pharmaceutical and biotech industries, the ultimate goal is better patient care.

5. Making connections and creating bonds

At a marketing association dinner, Curtis and Aldo are talking about the weather when Aldo mentions that the rain is affecting his golf game. The two men discover that they both enjoy golf, both live in the same neighborhood, and both have two boys under the age of five. They create a bond when they discover these similarities.

Humans are "hard-wired" to bond. This is a normal process, because bonding is one of life's more rewarding experiences. You may not be aware of bonding while it is happening, but you can tell when bonding doesn't take place because of the uneasiness or tension you feel.

Research shows that we like people who are like us. The old adage "opposites attract" may work for the initial stages of a relationship, but studies show that both business and personal relationships are more successful over the long term when people share similar values, experiences, goals and ideals. Sharing even superficial qualities such as age group and background can lead to stronger connections.

We like people who are like us because they feel comfortable and familiar. When people say, "I like you," they really mean, "I am like you." When you feel similar to someone, you experience warm feelings of rapport.

6. Getting in synch to establish rapport

When we feel rapport with someone, something interesting happens. We unconsciously synchronize our voices and body language. We do this without even being aware of it.

Synchronizing is nothing new. We have been synchronizing since birth by responding to feedback from our caregivers. When someone smiles at us, we instinctively smile back. If someone asks, "How are you today?" we parrot back, "Fine. How are you?" We naturally reciprocate behavior.

What about the real you? Are you being phony by adapting to others? The French have a saying: "A car could go just as far on square wheels as on round wheels. The difference is that on round wheels the ride is much, much smoother."

Do you know people who have trouble getting along with others? Chances are these people act the same way with everyone. They don't "read" other people well, and they are too inflexible to adapt their styles.

People who get along well with others behave a little differently with each person they meet. They aren't selling out, they are adapting to the situation. By making each person feel comfortable, they are going through life on round wheels instead of square ones.

7. Mirroring body language and voice

Do you talk with your hands? You may appear overly dramatic or emotional to a reserved person. Conversely, if you keep your arms glued to your sides, you'll appear stiff to a more outgoing person. You don't have to change your style completely, but slightly increasing or decreasing your movements will help you get in synch.

Subtly mirroring your speaking partner's movements and posture can be very powerful. If he stands up, you stand up. If he leans on a desk, you lean on something. When he is lounging leisurely, echo his posture by relaxing a bit.

Mirroring vocal style is amazingly subtle, and very easy to do. People tune in to you when you talk at the same rate as they do, because their rate of speech corresponds to their rate of thinking. Mirror their volume as well by speaking more loudly or softly. Mirroring a person's speech patterns creates a sense that you are on the same wavelength.

The key to mirroring body language is subtlety. You never want people to feel you are mimicking them. Wait a few seconds, and casually echo their movements.

8. The secret of every successful person

What does it take to be successful? People who achieve their dreams are not necessarily the most intelligent, hardworking, or attractive, but they have one common trait: they know how to get along with people.

We may get through life by stepping on others to get our way, or by acting as human doormats, but we damage other people's egos as well as our own. The secret to getting along with people is to understand and meet their needs. William James, the father of American psychology, wrote, "The deepest principle in human nature is the craving to be appreciated."

We all have the same basic needs: to have our physical and emotional needs met, and to feel important and worthwhile. Don't be fooled by someone's aloofness or self-contained manner. The most accomplished people are often the most needy, and are driven to achieve.

We like people who make us feel valued. When someone shows warmth and a sincere interest in you, you probably think, "What a wonderful person this is." Everyone is tuned to the radio station, WII-FM: "What's In It For Me?" Find out what each person wants the most, and help them get it.

connection capsule

At the core of any successful business relationship is trust and respect.

When a doctor has a prescribing decision to make between similar products of equal efficacy and safety, often he or she will choose the product based on their representative of preference. In a nutshell, the doctor prescribes when the drug is right for the patient, and the rep is right for the doctor.

— Cindy Bernstein, Manager
Product Market Research
Pfizer Canada

Chapter 2

NON-VERBAL COMMUNICATION

Sending the right message

Facial expression is human experience
rendered immediately visible.

– Edmund Carpenter

9. Why making connections is personal

Why do people fly half way across the world to meet, when a phone call, fax or e-mail convey the same information at a fraction of the cost? It's because we need to see, hear and touch the people we do business with. That's how we make personal connections.

When we meet someone new, we use all our senses to determine if we can trust them. We shake their hand, make eye contact, and spend time in their presence to see how they move and react. We need to understand and feel comfortable with people before we trust them with our business.

Your personal contact with a customer gives you a chance to show trustworthiness and reliability. Your facial expression, body language, and mannerisms should all support your message, and help your clients and colleagues feel confidence in you.

Personal contact also gives you the opportunity to observe people's body language. You can monitor when your message is getting through, when you need to take another approach, or even when to reschedule your meeting for another time.

10. How being congruent builds your credibility

Mindy is telling the company's sales representatives about a new product the company is launching. The product is critical to the success of the company, but the content is dry, and Mindy is exhausted from a week of meetings. After the session, a colleague asks Mindy if she realized she had been leaning against the lectern with her chin resting in her hand. What a message Mindy was sending to the audience about this exciting new product!

You build your credibility on your physical presence because people believe and remember what they see. Being congruent means your voice, body language and words all send the same message. If you say one thing, but your body language belies your words, people will be confused, and you will lose credibility.

The good news is that you can control what people see. The way you stand, walk, and move sends a message about your thoughts and feelings. The angle of your head, whether your shoulders are slumped or pulled back, and the way you gesture all speak volumes about you. Pay attention to the signals you send. To inspire confidence, your actions should support your words.

11. Show charisma from across the room

Have you noticed people who seem to have charisma, or presence? People who exude class and confidence invariably have great posture. They stand and walk tall.

Your posture makes a strong impression because people notice it from across the room. It involves the whole body, not just the small muscles. Good posture is associated with self-confidence and leadership ability. People with good posture are perceived to be interested and honest.

Poor posture, with slumped shoulders and a lowered head, is associated with a lack of self-confidence, leadership skills and interest. Moreover, people with poor posture are perceived to pay less attention to detail, and may be considered less reliable and capable.

Standing tall is almost a magic bullet because it can make anyone appear more self-confident. It is a particularly valuable tool for someone who is shorter than average, has a high or weak voice, is generally less physically attractive or can't afford a top-quality wardrobe.

 Good posture costs much less than a good suit – and gets you many of the same benefits.

12. Eliminate distracting behaviors

At a department meeting, Tom, a sales manager, is unconsciously clicking his pen. Sophie, a sales representative, opens her mouth to a wide yawn. Paul, a training manager, plays with his beard, and every so often scratches his elbow.

We may not be aware of our mannerisms, but other people are. We may scratch ourselves, bite or lick our lips, play with our hair, moustache or beard, pick our teeth or fingernails, tap our feet, adjust our glasses, click pens, or drum our fingers.

These unconscious mannerisms send the message that we are tired, bored or distracted. We can catch ourselves and eliminate distracting habits so we look poised and professional. Ask a trusted friend to help you identify your tics and twitches.

You can undercut your words with your body language. If you tap your pen when you speak, the person listening to you will remember your pen. Sit still so you won't create distractions.

Whatever you do, from adjusting your eyeglasses to handing out a business card, avoid abrupt, jerky movements that make you look nervous or awkward. To exude self-confidence, keep all your movements controlled and purposeful.

13. Observe and use facial expressions to connect

Maria is in a department meeting. Everyone is tense about a problem in the department, and Maria is afraid she will be put on the spot. Maria is wearing a turtleneck sweater, and slowly starts pulling the sweater higher until it covers her mouth. Clearly, Maria doesn't want to talk about the subject!

People's faces and actions often reveal more than they realize. When meeting with customers and colleagues, observe their expressions for clues to their moods and thoughts. A genuine smile or nod can show approval or agreement, but an awkward smile can indicate nervousness. Blinking and rapid eye movement can reveal tension. Someone who doesn't make eye contact with you may be distracted or concerned about something else, or may be upset by what you said.

Use your own facial expressions to connect with people. Show that you're paying attention by making eye contact, and allowing an emotional reaction to their words show on your face. Look alert, positive, enthusiastic, open and confident – ready for anything that comes your way.

14. Make eye contact for powerful communication

In North America, pupil-to-pupil eye contact is normal business practice. You must maintain eye contact to project trustworthiness. Avoiding eye contact may raise doubts about your credibility.

Strong eye contact projects self-confidence, and shows that you are interested and paying attention. It makes others feel important, and encourages trust and respect.

In professional situations where important information is being communicated, aim for eye contact 70-80 percent of the time.

Good eye contact does not mean boring into someone's pupils. Too much intensity can be uncomfortable. Take the pressure off by looking at the corner of the eye, the bridge of the nose, or the forehead. Move your eyes slowly to meet someone's gaze, and avoid jerky, abrupt movements.

If someone appears reluctant to make eye contact, for cultural or personal reasons, don't force your gaze on them. In some cultures, avoiding eye contact is a sign of respect. (See Chapter 8: Across Cultures for details on dealing with other cultures).

ADV TIP

Look into people's eyes long enough to notice their eye color. Then you'll be sure you have made eye contact.

15. How a great smile lights up the room, and opens doors

Karen, administrative assistant to the president of a large pharmaceutical company, has a warm, friendly smile for everyone. Always approachable, and a great listener, Karen has been instrumental in helping her boss stay in tune with the employees. Karen's welcoming personality has helped the president connect with employees at all levels of the organization.

It's almost impossible not to return a sincere, happy smile. Our emotional brain conditions us to react to a genuine smile by feeling that the person is trustworthy, likeable, caring and competent.

There are two pre-requisites for a smile to work. First, it has to be genuine, and second, it has to be appropriate. Smiling while delivering sad news makes you look like the village idiot.

A broad, open-mouthed smile, especially with lots of teeth showing, can seem insincere because it is easy to put on, or fake. The muscles of the mouth can be easily contracted, but the eyes are not as easily engaged. In a warm, genuine smile the mouth, jaw and eyes are involved. A relaxed smile has lips closed or parted slightly. Have a warm, steady gaze, and allow your eyes to crinkle at the corners.

Your smile conveys warmth, sincerity and genuine interest. What's more, studies show that people who smile more are considered to be more intelligent.

16. Why your handshake is the focal point of your greeting

We create emotional bonds through physical connection and close proximity. In most of North America, the handshake is the only time we allow strangers into our personal space, so it has taken on a lot of significance. The quality of someone's handshake influences our impression of them, and possibly our decisions about whether or not we will work with them.

The purpose of a handshake is to bond, so take the time to meet and greet someone properly. A rushed, limp, perfunctory or bone-crushing handshake doesn't help you get the relationship off to a good start.

 To show warmth, grip the person's hand a second longer than expected, and then let go. Try to be the last person to release the grip. Keep your motion smooth, and avoid vigorous pumping that can be distracting.

 The handshake is a powerful way to connect in business, so don't miss the opportunity to use it again when you part. A good-bye handshake can be even more valuable than an introductory one because it concludes your meeting on a warm note. Hold the handshake a split-second longer than before, as if to convey, "Now that I know you, I like and respect you even more." Even if an exchange hasn't gone as well as you had hoped, a parting handshake conveys the message that you still want to work together.

17. How to read people's body language

You're discussing your product with a physician. He seems to be absently nodding in agreement. Then he glances at his watch and picks up some charts on his desk.

The physician is sending a clear signal that he is uncomfortable or uninterested in what you are saying. To ignore his non-verbal cues and continue in the same manner would be disastrous. You have to find out where you lost him, and address the problem so you can re-connect. Try asking a good open-ended question, followed by a pause, to engage him in conversation.

Body language can be described as "open" or "closed." People display closed body language when they feel uncomfortable, uninterested or threatened. They withdraw or hide their bodies by using various stances and physical shields for protection. They may fold their arms over their chests, lean away from you, or pick up papers and hold them up in front of their chests.

Open body language welcomes interaction. It involves facing others squarely, eye to eye, and chest to chest – even heart to heart. When discussing your products, use open body language. Studies show that much more communication takes place between people who face each other squarely.

Once you've asked a thought-provoking question, close your mouth and count silently to ten, to give the physician time to think and respond.

18. How to stand close enough but not too close for comfort

Imagine this. You are at a national sales meeting, and see someone you know slightly. This person recognizes you, and approaches to speak with you. He keeps coming towards you. Suddenly your heart starts to beat a little faster, and you wonder what he's doing.

We all have an inborn "fight or flight" mentality. When a stranger comes too close we have to make an instant decision about whether this is a friend or a foe. If a stranger invades your personal space, your senses wake up as you try to figure out what to do next.

Generally North Americans and Europeans stand about three feet, or arm's length, apart. People in other cultures may stand closer or farther away. Coming too close may intimidate or threaten someone, while standing far apart may cause someone to think you are remote or unfriendly.

To create rapport in a business setting, keep an appropriate distance between you and the other person. Stand close enough to be personal, but not intrusive. If you notice someone is backing away from you, resist the impulse to move closer. Aim to make people feel comfortable by respecting their personal space.

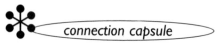

connection capsule

You build credibility when your body language matches your words.

To build good relationships with physicians, respect the inner workings of the office. Make appointments and abide by them. If you are changing positions, tell us who's replacing you and introduce them to us.

Don't demand to be seen. Don't be condescending and don't lecture us. Above all, don't negate other products, because doctors stop listening when you do this. If you constantly put down other companies, we take what you say with a grain of salt.

Be personable. Let us hear why your product is good. The sales representatives I like most to work with are the ones who keep me up to date with new studies, and have a positive attitude and outlook.

– Dyan Kimia, MDCM

Chapter 3

VOICE POWER

Speaking the language of success

Speak clearly, if at all; carve every word
before you let it fall.

– Oliver Wendell Holmes

19. Why voice quality is key to communication

Do you like the sound of your voice? Many people react negatively to their voices on a tape recorder, but otherwise don't pay much attention to their vocal qualities.

From the time we begin talking, most of us don't give much thought to our speech patterns. These patterns that we learned by imitating our families are strongly ingrained in us, but we may be completely unaware of how our voice sounds to others.

The voice communicates powerful messages. People react negatively to a variety of speech patterns, including voices that are nasal, whiny, monotonous, high-pitched, childlike, harsh, aggressive, mumbling, artificial, bossy, angry, defensive, sing-song, and very fast or very slow.

If you are concerned that your voice fits into any of these categories, you can improve your vocal quality by becoming aware of how you sound, and by learning a few simple techniques.

Your voice quality is a key to effective communication. People make assumptions about who you are by the way you sound. Your voice connects you to your audience on a visceral level and provides a foundation for building trust. When people trust you, they listen to you and are more willing to build a solid and productive relationship with you. A powerful and pleasant voice is worth cultivating.

20. Use vocal variety to communicate effectively

Voice pattern includes tone, pitch, rate of speech, diction, volume, accent and vocal variety. The first step to controlling your voice is to identify your vocal characteristics by listening to your voice mail message, or by asking a trusted friend or colleague for feedback.

Too much vocal variety sounds as if you are singing, but more people have the opposite problem – not enough variation. Monotonous voices trigger negative associations because they show no enthusiasm or emotion. They send the message that you are tired, apathetic or bored.

You want your voice to energize and motivate your customer or colleague into a new awareness. An expressive voice increases your chances of being listened to. People are more likely to hear and retain what you say, and you can communicate more complex ideas effectively.

Vary your volume, pace and inflection to suit the situation. At times, louder is better. At other times, quieter is more suitable. Sometimes silence is best of all. Variety breeds interest, believability and respect. With an adaptable voice you can use a slow, deliberate pace when needed, or speed up to make your point. The art of delivery is doing whatever it takes to be heard and understood at any given moment.

21. Adjust your volume and pitch for variety

Adjust your volume. Speaking too softly can be associated with a lack of self-confidence, shyness, nervousness and even dishonesty. In a one-to-one exchange, however, softer voices can be perceived as more friendly, approachable, humble and compassionate. Stronger volume reflects confidence, self-assurance, and leadership abilities, but if your voice is too loud it can be considered intimidating, rude and aggressive.

Vary your volume to suit the situation. When you speak to a crowd of 200 people, your volume will be stronger than when you have a private conversation in an office.

Adjust your pitch. Pitch is the highness or lowness of the voice, and it is the easiest way to add variety. Low-pitched voices are pleasing to the ear and are equated with trustworthiness and control. High-pitched voices are associated with strong emotions, and trigger associations of nervousness, agitation and lack of confidence.

 People who don't vary their pitch sound monotonous. You need a range of pitches for vocal interest. An easy exercise to increase your vocal pitch is to read a newspaper article using many pitch ranges. You'll get used to speaking in a greater range of pitches and have more vocal variety in your everyday speech.

22. Speed up or slow down to be understood

Sapandeep, a clinical research associate, was preparing to update the sales and marketing personnel on their Phase IV clinical trial. Normally a fast talker, Sapandeep's rate of speech increases when she's nervous. Combined with her accent, she can be difficult to understand. Her manager coached her before the presentation, and signaled her during the presentation whenever she needed to slow down. Once Sapandeep became aware of her speech patterns, she worked on modifying them. Her professional presentation at the district meeting raised her profile in the organization.

Many people feel compelled to fill every gap with conversation, and have developed a habit of talking too much and too quickly. People have to understand you in order to appreciate your ideas. Talking quickly adds energy to your voice, and conveys enthusiasm and commitment - up to a point. When people can't follow you or get a word in edgewise, they lose interest. If you talk quickly, slow down a bit. You'll appear more friendly, calm and approachable.

People who take forever to get their thoughts out can be equally frustrating. "Slow talkers" may appear tired or bored, or even self-absorbed. If you speak slowly, you may want to increase your speed, particularly when you're with a person who speaks quickly.

23. How to have the voice of authority

When physicians speak to patients, they are generally directive. They jump into the middle of a patient's description of pain to ask, "What kind of pain? Does it hurt here, or here?"

The person who directs the conversation is usually in a position of power in that relationship. The speaker feels authorized to control the flow of conversation, and she uses interruptions to manage the conversation, initiate topics and maintain the agenda.

Every conversation is a bit of a turf war. While one person speaks, the other waits to speak. Depending on the relationship and the situation, one person may have more power or control, and may use different language. In the traditional doctor/patient relationship, the doctor controls the agenda.

In *Power Talk* by Sarah Myers McGinty, controlling language is termed "Language from the Center." It is the voice of authority that is often the primary speech style of doctors, judges and police officers. This language style is useful for leading groups because it inspires trust, confidence and respect. But like any claim to power, it can lead to jealousy, resentment and competition.

24. Use the language of influence to build bridges

The patient answering the doctor is more likely to use "Language from the Edge." McGinty describes this as "careful, exploratory and inquiring." The speaker asks questions, reacts responsively and is deferential and collaborative. As with the patient meeting the doctor, people using language from the edge are listening, gathering information and learning, rather than directing. They defer power to the person with the knowledge.

When using this collaborative language you are perceived as approachable, personable and interested in others. You use active listening skills such as nodding when others speak, and asking for clarification. You respond rather than direct.

Language from the edge is used to influence rather than control. It gathers rather than presents information. It shows personal warmth, and cultivates the conversation. Use this language style when the process is more important than the turf. It creates bridges and invites interaction.

Choose your language style to suit the situation. You need a balance of styles to work in a variety of situations.

25. How to eliminate powerless phrases

Margaret, Vice President of Sales and Marketing, is giving an update on the pending product launch. The power of her voice is captivating. She stands tall, and speaks positively. She talks about the opportunity before them, and her confidence that they can make it happen.

Several years ago Margaret spoke with hesitancy. She hedged her phrases with, "I guess maybe we could..." Voice coaching helped her eliminate distracters in her speech, and learn how to use powerful language that projects authority and confidence.

Do you hedge your words with phrases such as, "I was wondering if we could..."? Do you use disclaimers such as, "I'm not sure I should bring this up, but..."? These speech patterns negate what follows, and project a lack of confidence.

Another language weakness is overusing modifiers, such as *very, really, many* and *certainly*. For example, "This is certainly the very very best drug in its class." Avoid cluttering your sentences and you'll communicate with more power.

Powerless language weakens our credibility, and can jeopardize our chances at being taken seriously. To sound more confident, replace, "I guess we could..." with, "We could..." As for disclaimers, you can eliminate those completely, and simply make your point.

26. How to use clear grammar to make a point

When we speak we have an intention in mind. Our message can be undermined by poor grammar or diction, or by using slang and fillers.

Work on cleaning up incorrect grammar, such as "He goes…" instead of "He said…" Clean up your diction as well. Diction is the way you say words. Saying *shoulda, wanna, otta, gonna, gotta, gimme,* sound less professional than *should have, want to, ought to, going to, have to, give me.*

Fillers such as *kinda, sorta* and *maybe* clutter up your language and distract people. Punctuating your speech with *um* and *uh* make you sound hesitant and unsure of yourself. Your listeners may end up counting the number of times you say, *uh* instead of listening to what you are saying.

The word *like* has become a multi-purpose filler. Saying, "It's, like, the best product in its class," does little to sell your product. Using high school language at work damages your credibility.

 To eliminate certain speech habits, you first have to become aware of them. Ask a friend to signal every time you say *uh*, or whatever your problem phrase may be. This may cause frustration at first, but once you become aware of your habits, you'll be able to break them.

27. Why 'not' to use negative language

When a doctor says, "This won't hurt a bit," what's the first thing the patient thinks? "This is going to hurt!" In order for our brain to process a negative, we first have to visualize the positive and then negate it. So when a doctor mentions "hurt," the patient is now focused on it because it entered his mind.

The negative "not" enters our minds unconsciously, and sends a clear signal that you have thought about what you are denying. For example, have you ever heard a pilot say "We are not anticipating any bad weather today, so you won't experience a bumpy ride." Bad weather? Bumpy ride? Now he's brought out all our fears and we're feeling nervous.

 Do you use unconscious negatives? When you tell your manager, "No problem" she hears "problem." Instead, how about saying "my pleasure"? Do you tell customers, "Please don't hesitate to contact me"? Hesitate? How about "Please contact me at any time."

Sales representatives who trash the competition leave a negative impression of themselves. It's acceptable to highlight differences in products, but you are challenging doctors' professional opinions when you speak negatively about products they use. Instead, highlight the benefits of your drug, and leave a positive impression of yourself.

We can train ourselves "not to speak in the negative."

28. How to use powerful words to connect

One of the most powerful triggers in the world is hearing your own name. When you hear your name in a crowded room, it catches your attention immediately. From the time you were a baby, you have heard your name and connected it to being the focus of someone's attention. Generally we feel pleasure when people turn their attention to us.

Using someone's name at the beginning or end of the sentence increases the likelihood that they will listen carefully. For example, "Jodie, can you have this report ready by this afternoon?" "Will you have time to look over this data, Dr. Smith?"

Now please consider the effect of a few more powerful words: "please" "thank you" and "consider". Mitsubishi Motors conducted a very successful advertising campaign based on the words "please" and "consider." Inviting someone to consider your idea is giving them a choice, and is one of the words least likely to provoke resistance. "Please" and "thank you" convey appreciation and gratitude. They are words we have been conditioned to use since childhood, and are linked with rewards and favors. Think about the simplicity and power of the following sentence:

"Dr. Smith, please consider Product X for your patients with Disease Y. Thank you."

connection capsule

The sound of your voice tells people who you are, and connects you with your listener.

The best way to build relationships with health care professionals is to be frank and honest, and to respect each other.

> – Denis Lacoste
> Clinical Science Associate
> Genzyme Canada Inc.

As a health care professional, I appreciate most working with sales representatives who transmit information with clarity and efficiency. This is especially important when the meeting occurs in a busy office.

> – Sophie Centazzo MD

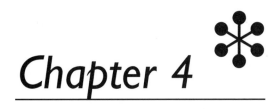

Chapter 4

LISTENING AND QUESTIONING

Keys to building understanding

When we speak with someone who pays close attention,
we instinctively give, rather than withhold.

– Janet MacPhee

29. Why active listening is vital to understanding

"Seek first to understand, then to be understood" is the Fifth Habit in Stephen Covey's book, *The 7 Habits of Highly Effective People*. While "hearing" is a passive activity, listening is a very active process that is hard work. This may explain why many people are not effective listeners. Listening is truly a gift you give to others. It is also a fundamental skill for successful selling.

Although we may want to listen effectively, it isn't always easy. Many of us aren't taught these skills, and distractions in our environment make it difficult to focus on what's being said. Phones ringing, people interrupting us, and mental or physical fatigue can all make active listening a challenge. To overcome these barriers, you first have to identify them. Then you can develop strategies for dealing with them, since most of the time you can't make these barriers go away.

Successful selling is based on effective listening. Developing your listening skills is a life-long process. When you interact with customers, listen carefully to uncover their needs. Understanding your customers' points of view will help you build trust that leads to long-term relationships.

30. How to listen actively and communicate your understanding

There are different levels of listening. At one level you concentrate on the person's words, and what they mean to you. As you listen more carefully, you'll note the person's body language and tune in to their emotions. Consider listening to be a whole-body process. Listen with your ears, watch for visual cues with your eyes, and use your heart to tune in to the emotional message the person is sending.

As you listen, you want to communicate your understanding so people know that their message is getting through. In order to communicate your understanding, use two techniques: empathizing, or clarifying by paraphrasing.

You empathize by putting yourself in the customer's shoes, and being sensitive to the feelings the customer expresses or implies. Empathizing creates rapport, opens the lines of communication and encourages discussion and further sharing.

Paraphrasing involves rewording what the customer tells you, using your own words. Begin with a statement such as, "If I understand you correctly..." Follow with a short question to check for understanding, such as, "Is that correct?" or "Is that what you mean?" By clarifying, you give customers the opportunity to correct any misunderstandings, and you show that you are listening and interested in what they are saying.

31. The power of questions to move people towards action

People believe 70% more of what they say than what you say. That's why questions are so powerful.

When you are selling, asking your customers questions that identify their needs and "hurts" is more effective than data dumping. Effective questions help you gather information so you know how to focus your discussion, and how to address your customers' concerns. This pays off in increased sales.

Even more important, questions engage customers by getting them involved and participating in a two-way conversation. By asking the right questions, you can get your customers to work with you towards resolving their concerns or conflicts. When they come up with the strategies, they are much more likely to implement them because they had input in creating them. In other words, they won't argue with their own data!

The person who asks the questions controls and directs the conversation. Before you meet with customers, plan your questions so they elicit information, and don't provoke defensive reactions. Effective questions help you to:

- Gather information
- Clarify points of view
- Identify needs
- Bring out concerns and problems
- Build trust and rapport

32. How to ask "open" and "closed" questions

Pamela is meeting with Dr. Smith to detail Product X. She asks Dr. Smith, "Do you prescribe Product X for your patients with Disease Y? Dr. Smith answers, "No." She tries another tactic. "Dr. Smith, what criteria do you use in choosing a product for treating Y?" Dr. Smith now describes her treatment choices, and opens up the discussion.

Open questions lead to descriptive answers. They start with "what", "when", "who", and "how". They ask for facts, explanations, or further details, and encourage customers to express themselves. Open questions provide you with more information, so you don't have to ask as many questions. They involve the customer, and convey your willingness to listen.

Closed questions start with "do" (Do you...? Did you...?), and can be answered with one word: "yes" or "no." They can limit or end the conversation.

Closed questions are effective for gathering factual information and for focusing the customer in a specific direction, especially if the customer is talkative and you have limited time together. You can use closed questions such as "How much...?" or "Can you...?" to complete the information gathered from the open-ended questions.

33. Why asking "why" questions may not get you the results you want

John, a district manager, is waiting for a report from Cynthia, a product manager. John asks Cynthia, "Why is it taking you so long to complete that report?" John shouldn't be surprised to get a defensive reaction from Cynthia, who now feels as if she has to justify her behavior. When John later apologizes for his confrontational approach, they explore the situation together and John realizes that Cynthia has legitimate reasons for the report being late.

Asking "why" may get you more information, but it can also evoke defensive reactions. People may feel that you are criticizing them or being confrontational, and feel compelled to justify their behavior. "Why" questions may also be seen as aggressive or threatening, and you are less likely to get the information and cooperation you want.

Compare these questions. Chances are you'd receive a more open response to the second version of each question.

1. Why did it take you so long to complete the report?

   What caused the completion of the report to take longer than anticipated?

2. Why haven't you prescribed our products before?

   What features and patient benefits are most important to you?

34. Dos and don'ts for effective questions

Avoid:

✘ Multiple or compound questions that cause confusion. An example is, "What do you think of our efficacy data, the extensive clinical support we have for this product, and the fact that it is on the hospital formulary?"

✘ "Leading", "loaded" or "suggestive" questions. These questions encourage customers to tell you what you want to hear, not necessarily what they are thinking or feeling. An example is, "You know the correct dosing for Product X, don't you Doctor Smith?"

Do:

✔ Plan your questions. Know what you will ask and why you are asking it.

✔ Know when to stop asking questions. Watch for signs of discomfort or impatience.

✔ Ask sensitive questions last, and only if you have established rapport.

connection capsule

Remember the 80/20 rule: your customers should be speaking 80 percent of the time.

When you meet with the physician, reverse roles and listen more than you speak. Let the physician open up and talk about his concerns. Then lead with your best punch. In a short call, don't try to sell your whole presentation module. Distill your message and present two or three facts so you can leave the physician satisfied, not confused.

– Alfred Balbul, M.D. C.S.P.Q., F.R.C.P.(C)

Building relationships begins with a commitment to quality service. Through respect for people and collaboration these relationships can continue to flourish.

– Wayne Hartman
Sales Training and Development
Wyeth Canada

Chapter 5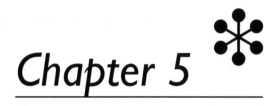

EMOTIONAL INTELLIGENCE

Building positive relationships with clients and colleagues

Your relationship with your customer is not based just on how smart you are. It's based on how the customer feels about doing business with you.

– Diane Bussandri

35. Why EQ may be more valuable than IQ

At ABC Pharmaceuticals, David has it; Dennis doesn't. Both men are managers. David has an extensive and impressive network of relationships. He is constantly in contact with people, including company employees, suppliers, customers and colleagues in other organizations.

People are comfortable with David and they trust him. He listens to them, tries to understand their perspectives, and builds on their ideas. He is collaborative and inclusive. He also manages himself well. He's in touch with his own feelings and can motivate himself. Even in difficult situations he usually finds the drive and energy for new assignments and responsibilities. He can make tough, unpopular decisions, but always explains his rationale and communicates his plans.

Dennis is technically brilliant and comes up with many ideas, but co-workers wouldn't describe him as a "people person." Everyone in the office recognizes his bad days. He's moody, doesn't pick up on cues from others, and pushes his agenda in meetings without listening to anyone else. He's solitary and thinks networking is a waste of time. He says, "If people spent as much time working as they do talking to each other, we would get a lot more done."

On IQ tests, Dennis measures higher than David. But David's EQ, or emotional intelligence, is much higher. The subject of EQ isn't new, but we are becoming more and more aware of its impact on the health of organizations.

36. What is emotional intelligence?

Emotional intelligence is about managing our emotions and recognizing emotions in others so that we can build positive, long-term relationships. Daniel Goleman, author of *Working with Emotional Intelligence,* defines EQ this way: "We're being judged by a new yardstick; not just by how smart we are, or by our training and experience, but by how well we manage ourselves and each other."

The five key components of emotional intelligence are:

1. **Knowing your emotions:** recognizing a feeling as it is happening to you

2. **Managing your emotions:** handling your feelings so that you are in control, and not a victim of your emotions

3. **Motivating yourself:** using your emotions to help you reach your goal, to keep focused, to delay gratification and to stifle impulsiveness

4. **Recognizing emotions in others:** understanding what is happening to another person at an emotional level, and demonstrating empathy

5. **Building relationships:** using these skills to connect to others in a meaningful way, to enhance your interpersonal effectiveness

37. How EQ helps the bottom line

"Only 15 percent of one's financial success is due to technical knowledge." This was written by Dale Carnegie in 1936, and holds true today.

The way we behave at work has a big impact on the success of our organization because organizations get things done through people. Here's how employee behavior affects your company:

Customer service: Statistics show that up to 70 percent of customers stop doing business with a company for EQ-related reasons. People buy from a person, not from a company. In pharmaceutical sales, when several drugs are of equal efficacy, physicians buy from the sales representative with whom they have the best relationship.

Conflict resolution: EQ isn't about being nice. Emotionally intelligent people can disagree with team members, and debate ideas. The result is improved products and customer service.

Hiring and placement: Managers with high levels of EQ can recognize and select employees with high EQ and place them in their optimal positions. Many human resource professionals say, "If you have to hire just one attribute, make it emotional intelligence."

Employee retention and satisfaction: Emotionally intelligent managers help employees feel respected, acknowledged, supported and appreciated. When employees feel valued they don't leave.

38. How to identify your feelings so you can deal with them

Are you able to describe how you feel? To many people, defining and describing their emotions is a mystery. We may say we are fed up when we're actually disappointed, or that we feel upset when we're really feeling embarrassed.

The first step towards identifying your emotions is building vocabulary that expresses your feelings. Describe as precisely as possible how you feel. Are you feeling frustrated, angry, or despondent? You have to be able to label your feelings clearly before you can react appropriately.

Next, identify the cause of the feelings. Think about what happened before you felt this way. Then ask yourself if your emotional state is appropriate to the situation.

Remember that every emotion is valid. The first step towards building emotional intelligence is learning to identify your feelings.

39. How to manage your feelings

Richard, new to the team, is meeting with his boss and colleagues. He offers his opinion on the new marketing campaign and immediately regrets it. His boss dismisses his suggestion in mid-sentence and says that he is looking for "breakthrough" ideas. Richard physically pulls back from the table, crosses his arms and remains quiet for the rest of the meeting.

How would you feel and act if you were Richard? Here are the key steps in managing your feelings:

1. **Identify your emotions** and the cause of the feelings.

2. **Ask what would help you feel better.** Don't assume that the way you feel is the way it has to be. You can regulate your moods and feelings by what you say to yourself.

3. **Generate options for your response**. If you were Richard, would it be best to withdraw from the conversation or to stay involved? Could you speak to your boss privately, get involved in the meeting in some other way, or present your ideas differently at the next meeting? Sometimes the ideas you generate can help you see things in a different light.

4. **Consider your options** and choose the best one.

5. **Learn to control the intensity** of certain emotions. That doesn't mean you should not reveal your feelings, but your workplace relationships won't thrive if your boss and colleagues think of you as sulky, timid or thin-skinned.

40. How to change your behavior: the 21-day rule

Do you have an aspect of emotional intelligence that you would like to enhance? Begin by identifying a behavior you would like to change. For example, if your typical reaction to new ideas is to reject them, you can choose to be more open to suggestions. You can decide to listen more closely and not say anything until you've thought about it.

Changing behavior takes time and involves strong motivation, but research shows that if you stick to a new behavior for 21 days, it becomes incorporated into your everyday actions. To change your behavior:

- Select a behavior you want to change.
- Make it specific and clear.
- Make it measurable.
- Practice it every day.
- Make it something you want to do.
- Take full power and responsibility for your actions.

To help you develop new behavior, the buddy system can be invaluable. Ask a friend or colleague at work for feedback. Choose someone who has good EQ and can support you, confront you and challenge you.

Remember that emotional intelligence is multi-layered and complex. We never "arrive". Fatigue or frustration may derail us from time to time. Building EQ is a lifelong task. Stay focused. It's worth it.

> *connection capsule*

There's a direct correlation between your level of emotional intelligence and your success at work.

The best way to build successful relationships is by using the Golden Rule. "Treat others as you want to be treated," with the utmost in professionalism, honesty, integrity and respect for their culture, needs and time. Let the health care professional get to know the "real you" and how much you are committed to meeting their needs. If you enjoy what you do and make every encounter meaningful, they will enjoy supporting you and contributing to your success.

– Gayle Waylett, R.D.N., MPH
Western Regional Sales Manager
Novartis Nutrition Corporation

Chapter 6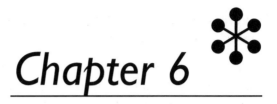

RESOLVING CONFLICT

Strategies for defusing conflict and turning relationships around

Conflict presents us with fantastic opportunities to create greater understanding between people, get more of our needs met, and forge new alliances.

– Frema Engel

41. Why conflict is a natural by-product of workplace relationships

The sales of a new product are falling short of expectations and tension is high. Sales management attributes this problem to a poorly planned marketing campaign, and a visual aid too long and complicated to use effectively. Product management says the sales representatives aren't following the marketing plan and are communicating the wrong message to their customers. They say the representatives were not properly trained to use the visual aid.

A conflict-free workplace is unrealistic. When people with different points of view, feelings, life experiences or needs interact, conflict often results. Most conflicts start over a mis-communication, a comment causing hurt feelings, or a misunderstanding. Things grow out of proportion because both parties think they're right and neither wants to back down.

Most people think conflict is something to avoid. This is not necessarily true. When we know how to deal with conflict, it can be a great motivator for change. The key is to face the situation and find workable solutions.

42. Working together to create winning conditions

Beth, Vince and Jill are sales representatives with Pharmaceuticals Inc. They call on the same physicians but sell different products. Beth and Vince communicate regularly and share information about their mutual customers. They both feel that Jill is slacking off. Jill says that Beth and Vince's meetings are a waste of time, so she refuses to participate. Instead of collaborating with Beth and Vince, Jill is competitive and hostile. The team's productivity is rapidly declining.

The three sales representatives need to collaborate and exploit their strengths to meet their customers' needs. Either Beth or Vince could approach Jill to find out her side of the story, and discuss how they can pull together to meet their customers' needs.

It takes two people to start a conflict, but one person to take steps to resolve it. We each have a choice. We can be critical and blaming, or constructive and understanding. Sometimes the solutions aren't as important as everyone feeling heard, understood and respected. With a positive approach, we can usually disarm even a critical and negative person, and begin a dialogue.

43. How to defuse conflict and build consensus

How do you react when you're in conflict with colleagues? Do you ignore the issue? Do you become paralysed if they become angry, hostile, or rude to you? Do you become aggressive and try to impose your will on them?

Disputes are emotional. In arguments about minor issues, our emotional levels are generally low. When we feel passionate about an idea or our well-being is threatened, our emotions rise. The more intensely we feel about issues, the more emotional we become and the more we fight to safeguard our positions.

Conflicts make us unhappy. They use up time and energy, and disrupt our lives. They affect our sleep, relationships, productivity, and even the way we see the world. Many people get depressed because of long-standing disputes.

| A D V |
| T I P |

Pride often stops us from taking the first step. Many people see this as giving in - a sign of weakness or failure. Actually it's a sign of power. It takes more strength, thought, and willpower to resolve a conflict than to perpetuate it.

People who are consensus builders understand the importance of dealing with issues head on, clearing up misunderstanding, and resolving disputes. When you learn how to build consensus with colleagues and customers, you'll be in a unique position, and be looked upon as a leader.

44. How to take charge of your own emotions

No one likes to acknowledge the darker side of their personality, yet we all have moments when we lose it. How do you behave when you are overly stressed, anxious, or frustrated? Do you take out your anger on others? Do you hold a grudge? Do you perpetuate a less-than-satisfactory relationship?

Work on developing a greater understanding of your strengths and weaknesses. Examine the issues that are bothering you and figure out a plan to handle them.

Taking charge of your emotions means dealing with your feelings, especially negative ones. Negative feelings lead to negative behaviours and then to negative actions. Harness those negative emotions and transform them into positive, welcoming behaviours.

45. Five steps to resolving conflicts

The key to dealing with high emotional levels is to defuse the anger and begin a dialogue.

1. Make the first move. Suggest having coffee or lunch together to try to resolve the misunderstanding.

2. Invite the person to speak first. Find out why they feel wronged. Listen attentively, and you'll hear feelings come through. Acknowledge those feelings. Most people are more cooperative when they feel heard, understood, or have their concerns validated.

3. Speak in a calm voice. Explain your needs, feelings and interests. Stick to the issues and avoid being critical or judgmental of the person.

4. Try to agree on small issues before you tackle the big problem. Propose solutions that show flexibility.

5. Talk about what you've achieved through the conversation and decide on the next steps. If you've cleared the air and agreed to work on solutions, then you're both winners. So is your company.

46. Stopping hostility, rudeness or unacceptable behaviour

Pat, a colleague, frequently interrupts you in team meetings. How do you handle a colleague who belittles you or cuts you off in meetings? What do you do when you encounter stony silence, rudeness or an unwillingness to discuss an issue?

If you don't feel good about the way someone treats you, you need to approach the person and stop the behaviour. Here's how you could apply the steps to resolving conflict with Pat.

Approach Pat and say, "This morning in the meeting you raised your voice at me and interrupted me twice. Perhaps you're not aware of what you're doing, but this has happened before. I don't appreciate it and I'd like you to please stop."

This should elicit an apology. But what if Pat argues, becomes defensive or goes on the attack? Invite Pat to go for coffee. Explain your problem in a calm voice, and ask for input on how to resolve the issue. When you speak firmly and with respect, you will most likely clear the air and improve your relationship.

We don't usually view conflict as positive. Yet conflict can generate new ideas, learning, growth and positive energy. We can use these forces to build relationships, improve productivity, and enhance our performance. The key is learning how to deal with conflict.

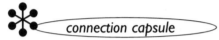

connection capsule

You can use conflict as a catalyst for change.

The best way to build relationships with health–care professionals is to truly care for them and to genuinely understand their needs and issues. It then becomes second nature to propose alternatives or solutions that will make a real difference for them.

> – Chantale Fortin, Quebec Regional Manager
> Specialty Sales Force, Sanofi-Synthelabo

Chapter 7

CUSTOMER CARE

Working with health care professionals and staff

Ask what your customers want and expect
from you before your competitors do.

– Patricia Fripp

47. Impressing the "Director of First Impressions"

Mitch, a new sale representative, has an appointment with Dr. Frank. Mitch announces himself to the receptionist, and sits down in the waiting room. After a few minutes, the receptionist tells Mitch that the doctor has been delayed, and asks if he would like to reschedule the appointment. Mitch impatiently informs her that he had an appointment at 2:00, and doesn't have time to come back.

Do you think the receptionist will go out of her way to fit Mitch into the next available slot? Not likely. And if Mitch does get to see the doctor, what do you think the receptionist will say about him to the doctor?

Although receptionists are often referred to as the gatekeepers, think of them as "Directors of First Impressions" for the doctor. Receptionists have to deal with hectic schedules and difficult bosses, as well as frustrated and sick patients. If you make their day more difficult by acting pushy or condescending, they are more likely to deny you access to the physician.

Treat receptionists with the utmost consideration and respect. You will stand out from the crowd, and be remembered for your courtesy and professionalism. And when the receptionist sees a window in the doctor's schedule, she will be much more likely to squeeze you in – perhaps ahead of your competitor.

48. How to develop warm relationships with staff

Kimberly, a sales representative, often brings muffins and coffee to early morning sales calls. What's more, for each office she visits she remembers who likes milk, cream, or sugar in their coffee. She is always greeted by a warm smile when she arrives.

Building relationships with members of the staff can reap big rewards for you. In *The Doctor as Customer,* Dr. Andy Farah says, "Locate the key person in that office. Is it the receptionist? The office manager? The staff controls access, and they often view themselves as protectors of the physicians' time. It's always a good idea to consider the staff members as customers too. For all practical purposes, you are in the position of selling them on you. Successful representatives know that their real mission is to keep the receptionists happy."

Spend a few minutes learning the names of the office staff. Notice the pictures on their desks, and ask about their children or hobbies. Don't try to fake a relationship by aggressively pursuing rapport. Showing genuine interest and respect for office staff will help you break through the barriers that keep you from the doctor. Work with the staff, and they will become champions of you and your products.

49. Office etiquette for a total office call

Your parents may have taught you etiquette, but they probably didn't teach you the unspoken rules of pharmaceutical sales etiquette. Your goal is to make a great first impression by showing respect and consideration for others, and by understanding the rules of each institution.

Each physician has a unique policy about sales representatives' visits. In some offices you will have to work harder at building relationships than in others. You'll find that the more value you bring to their medical practices, the greater access you'll get to the physician.

You may encounter patients who resent your getting in to see the doctor ahead of them. The solution is to practice prevention by having an appointment. If patients make negative remarks, it's important to empathize. Say something like, "I can understand how frustrated you feel. I have an appointment with Dr. White, and it will only take 10 minutes." Keep your voice calm, and focus on the reason you are seeing Dr. White – to educate her on the latest information, so she can give the best possible care to her patients.

50. Hospital etiquette that sets you above the crowd

A district sales manager and a newly promoted hospital representative are on their way to see a key opinion-leading physician. They enter a crowded elevator and the sales representative comments, "I heard Dr. G is a real jerk." Imagine their chagrin when, moments later, they enter Dr. G's office and realize that he was standing next to them in the elevator - wearing casual clothes.

Here are some tips for better hospital behavior:

- Study the layout of the hospital so you don't find yourself wandering in areas restricted to hospital staff.

- Treat everyone with respect, from the CEO to the cleaning staff. You never know who can help you find your way around. And you never know who's standing beside you in the elevator or in the cafeteria line.

- Check with the pharmacy first to find out the policy on visiting health care professionals in the hospital.

- Carry only a small briefcase and keep your detail bag locked in your car. You don't need the samples anyway as most hospital policies do not allow you to leave samples.

- If you are allowed to set up a small counter-top display in the hospital, be careful that you do not inadvertently promote your products to patients.

51. How to show grace under fire

Carlos has been waiting at a drop-in medical clinic to see a high-prescribing physician in his territory. After a while, he checks with the receptionist to see when the doctor will be available and learns that the doctor has slipped out the back door of the clinic. No one bothered to tell him.

Have you experienced anything similar? Or, perhaps you've been on the receiving end of a physician's or nurse's disparaging comments about your company, or pharmaceutical representatives in general.

How do you handle these stressful situations on the job? With poise and professionalism. If you wasted your time waiting for a physician, chalk it up to experience. Next time plan a different approach, such as inviting that physician to a Continuing Medical Education (CME) event.

If someone makes a negative remark, although it's difficult to do, try not to take it personally. The physician may be having a difficult day and you happened to be there at the wrong time. Don't try to give him information when he's too distracted to listen. Empathize, and ask if there's anything you can do for him. He'll be more likely to see you the next time.

52. How to get the most from your face-to-face time with a physician

Face-to-face time with physicians is continually shrinking. Once you gain access the first time, it's vital to connect so you get repeat access. In *The Doctor as Customer*, Dr. Andy Farah says, "Your first priority should be building relationships with your physician customers. When you walk in, you want to be greeted as a friend, not just another rep."

You've probably heard of the 80/20 rule. In a sales call, the physician should be talking 80 percent of the time. For most representatives it's the reverse. Avoid a "data dump" of product information, and listen instead. Encourage physicians to express their needs. After all, how can you provide a solution without identifying the problem?

Do some research into the physician's background. Refer to previous call notes. Ask the receptionist when the physician prefers to see representatives, and about the physician's attitude towards your products. When possible, diplomatically ask which samples they distribute to patients the most. Knowing what kind of information to provide will help you build long-term relationships.

ADV TIP

Are you upholding the 80/20 rule? It takes 21 days to form a new habit, so on your next 21 calls, become more conscious of who is doing most of the talking. If it's you, try to talk less, and ask and listen more.

53. How to connect with "hard-to-see" doctors

Time is precious for everyone, but particularly for physicians who are taking time away from patients to see you. Before visiting a physician's office, decide if this is a worthwhile target. Gather information from prescription data, and from the local pharmacy about the physician's preferences. Also check with your manager and other sales representatives. Not every doctor's office in your territory is a primary target.

For offices that work on a drop-in basis, introduce yourself to the nurse or receptionist. Present your card and the name of your products, and ask if you can see the doctor. Always be courteous and professional. If the physician is not available, arrange for a better time to come back.

If the office staff tells you that the physicians at this clinic don't see sales representatives, ask how the physicians prefer to be contacted. Do these physicians attend satellite conferences or other CME events? Could they be seen at the hospital? Are they interested in receiving current clinical studies? Would they be interested in participating in a clinical trial? Would they be willing to act as CME facilitators or moderators?

You can also use mailings and entertainment events to connect with physicians, as long as they comply with your company's guidelines. Use your creativity to make a connection.

54. How to say "no" to demanding behavior

Physicians are intelligent and highly educated. They can be very rewarding to work with, but some can be extremely demanding. Physicians may ask to fly first class to meetings, and to bring their spouse and children to CME events at your expense. They may expect you to order the best wine on the menu.

We realize that our industry has created this situation, but times are changing. The pharmaceutical industry is policing itself in an attempt to bring these situations under control. In the meantime, front line sales representative are in the awkward position of having to say "no" where they said "yes" in the past. Fortunately, national medical associations also see the need to control excessive spending.

As a sales representative, explain to the physician that your company complies with industry guidelines, and that as an employee you must follow your company's directives. Mention that the purpose of this self-policing effort is to limit further government intervention down the road.

If the physician continues to pressure you, say that you need to speak with your manager to see if a compromise can be worked out. This gives you time to think, regroup and strategize with your manager about how to deal with this physician's demands.

55. How to deal with abusive behavior

Joan has been calling on Dr. C for two years. His behavior is making her feel increasingly uncomfortable. It began when Dr. C suggested jokingly that he might prescribe her product more often if the company would send them to a beach resort together so he could see her in a bikini. On her last visit, Dr. C positioned himself much too close for comfort. Joan didn't want to make a big deal about it and remained quiet. However, now she prefers not to call on Dr. C at all.

Sexual remarks from prescribing customers or colleagues are unacceptable. Verbal abuse is also unacceptable. For example, a physician may become angry at not receiving a grant for clinical research, and make offensive remarks about you and your company.

If you have experienced aggressive or insulting behavior, speak to your manager. Ask for help in working out a strategy to deal with it. Companies value their employees and don't want them to be the innocent recipients of abusive behavior. No customer or colleague has the right to demean or belittle you. Assertively state that you are not required to put up with that behavior. But before walking out, say that you would be willing to continue the discussion when the person treats you respectfully.

56. Selling to customers who have become your friends

If you're in the enviable position, from the perspective of newly hired representatives, of being regarded by the doctor as a friend. So how do you ask for the business without jeopardizing the relationship?

The key is to take your conversations to a deeper level. Instead of discussing the physicians' golf games or vacations for the entire call, prepare open-ended questions. Ask their opinions about the latest treatments for diseases where your product is used. Use questions to uncover challenges these physicians are facing, or offer to search the literature for answers to their problems. Also, explore ways to help these physicians achieve their goals by asking other physicians you call on about their experiences. You can share the ideas you receive with your valued customers.

Use your strong connections to leverage your relationship with these physicians. Offer them opportunities to act as a chairperson for a CME event, or offer them training in facilitating small-group learning events with other physicians. You can also enlist their help by asking them to discuss with their colleagues the successes they've had with your products.

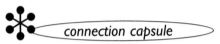
connection capsule

Customer access is based on customer relationships.

To market to physicians, you want to influence us and present new information without lecturing or acting pushy. We have been lectured to all our lives, and don't want to be lectured to by pharmaceutical representatives!

Instead, show sensitivity to us and to the office staff. Build relationships by getting to know the staff on a first name basis. Ask them when is the best time to see the doctor. Is it in the morning? At lunchtime? Bring the staff sandwiches or chocolate. You want them to be working with you, not against you.

– Alfred Balbul, M.D. C.S.P.Q., F.R.C.P.(C)

Chapter 8

ACROSS CULTURES
Meeting the foreign-born physician

To know another's language and not his culture is a quick way to make an intelligent fool of yourself.

– Anonymous

57. How to connect with foreign-born physicians

Jason, a senior sales representative, prides himself on his excellent rapport with physicians in his territory. At his first appointment with Dr. Warnakulasuriya, Jason greets him with a hearty handshake and addresses the doctor by name. In doing so he mispronounces the doctor's name. He enters the doctor's office and makes himself comfortable in the nearest chair. He attempts to break the ice by asking about the doctor's weekend. The doctor barely responds, so Jason asks about his practice and prescribing habits. Dr. Warnakulasuriya answers in monosyllables. Jason leaves feeling frustrated, wondering why he had so much trouble connecting.

Jason's natural style in dealing with physicians didn't work with Dr. Warnakulasuriya. He misread the cultural clues, and both men felt uncomfortable. Jason's firm handshake was more than this doctor was used to. By sitting down without being invited, Jason acted too casually, too quickly. He also should have checked with the receptionist to make sure he pronounced the doctor's name correctly.

 Even if you're an experienced sales representative, you may need to adapt your behavior when dealing with physicians from other cultures. Don't rush the process. Be polite and formal until you get to know each other better. Take time to build relationships before you attempt to sell your products.

58. How to avoid misunderstandings

Which of these scenarios sound familiar to you when dealing with foreign-born physicians?

- I have difficulty creating rapport and making small talk.

- I'm not sure how to establish a trusting relationship.

- Foreign-born physicians don't appreciate my attempts at humor.

- I've made a faux pas, but I don't know what I did wrong.

- It's difficult to get commitment. The physician doesn't react in the way I expect.

Communication techniques that work with physicians from your own culture may lead to miscommunication when you interact with physicians from other cultures. To connect with foreign-born customers, you need to understand and be respectful of their cultures.

ADV TIP

North America's business style is casual and direct. We make eye contact, shake hands firmly, and get down to business after a few minutes of small talk. Many cultures have a more conservative approach to social and business behavior, and take much longer to build relationships before conducting business. Err on the side of formality. Show that you are sincerely interested in developing long-term relationships. When you take a gradual, respectful approach you will be viewed as a skilled, dignified business professional.

59. How head-to-head comparisons can cause you to lose your toehold

Lisa is a new rep who has been on territory for three months. This is her first call on Dr. Khan. Lisa is keen to make the sale, and her objective is to convince Dr. Khan that her product is superior to the competition's product.

Lisa probes Dr. Khan with direct and open-ended questions to find out her prescribing habits. When Dr. Khan mentions that she prescribes the competitor's product and that her patients are doing very well on it, Lisa pulls out head-to-head comparisons. By this time, Dr. Khan is frowning, and Lisa wonders what went wrong.

Lisa's tactics would be poorly viewed by most physicians, and are particularly offensive to foreign-born physicians. Physicians from other cultures view direct questioning, debating the doctor, making head-to-head comparisons and attacking the competition as boastful and overly confident.

Doctors are trained to have the final say and the right answer. In debating Dr. Khan, Lisa is challenging her medical expertise and knowledge, and implying that Dr. Khan is not practicing the best medicine. Most doctors prefer a more collaborative approach.

If you were raised outside of North America, be conscious of how your selling techniques may be viewed differently when you call on North American physicians.

60. How to keep good communication from going sour

When you communicate with foreign-born physicians, are you conscious of how differently they may perceive you, compared with physicians from your own culture?

Foreign-born physicians may consider North American business conduct to be inappropriate. In cultures that place a high value on harmonious relationships, courtesy and sensitivity are paramount. Acting impatiently and addressing a business issue too early in the relationship may be considered rude or offensive.

 North Americans prize independence and individual achievement. In other cultures it is more important to show deference and respect for authority. In Asian cultures, for example, preserving "face," or preventing someone from "losing face" is very significant. When you argue with an Asian physician, your behavior may be perceived as offensive.

Always remain respectful. You can agree that other drugs can be appropriate, while pointing out that your product can provide an alternative. Show patience and continue to build rapport, with the goal of long term-relationships rather than short-term sales.

61. How to make sure your message is received and understood

Patrick presents a new drug to Dr. Lopez, and Dr. Lopez nods his head. When Patrick asks, "Do you understand?" Dr. Lopez looks insulted.

When we deal with other cultures, ensuring comprehension and getting feedback is different from what we expect. Here are some tips for better interaction:

- People may avoid asking questions because they believe it implies the speaker hasn't been clear, or they aren't intelligent enough to understand what you said. Check for comprehension by asking, "Am I explaining myself well?" instead of "Do you understand?" which can be considered impolite.

- In some cultures it is considered rude to interrupt a speaker to ask a question. Pause and give people a chance to ask questions.

- Nodding "yes" can mean "I hear you" rather than "I agree with you." It can even mean "no" or "maybe." Body language may not convey what you think it does. Learn the cultural nuances of your customers.

- Use visual aids to reinforce your message. Present material in smaller segments to allow for questions and reactions.

- Give an overview of your topic and summarize each topic before you move on. And if you are selling in a physician's office, you have to do all this in three minutes or less!

62. Good communication that helps you get to first base

Phillip, a senior hospital representative, meets with Dr. Tanaka to ask her to act as a chairperson for a CME event. When Dr. Tanaka agrees to become involved, Phillip says, "Great! Let's take the ball and run with it." Dr. Tanaka gives him a puzzled look.

Anita, a new representative, greets a foreign-born receptionist with, "What's up?" The receptionist glances at the ceiling. When Anita mentions that she's been tied up at the office, the receptionist wonders what exactly is going on at her company.

North Americans use slang and jargon all the time. Sports jargon is particularly prevalent. Expressions like, "I can't get to first base with that guy," are commonly used. These expressions hinder communication because they are culturally based, and are not necessarily understood by someone whose native language isn't North American English. Even people from India or Pakistan, whose first language is English, may find North American expressions virtually incomprehensible.

Avoid slang and idiomatic expressions. Don't make the mistake of speaking more loudly to someone whose first language isn't English, or even to someone who is fluent in English but from another culture. They aren't hard of hearing - they are just unfamiliar with your expressions. For clear communication, speak more slowly, and use formal, simple and polite language.

63. Small talk that connects across cultures

Mike meets several foreign-born physicians at a CME event and attempts to engage them in small talk. He begins with, "Did you see the game last night?" Mike receives blank looks, so he decides to tell a joke. His listeners don't react.

We may not initially realize that many cultures are not as sports-oriented as North Americans are, and it's not always a good subject for small talk. Telling jokes is equally tricky, because humor is culturally based. Even the most innocent joke may be misunderstood by someone from another culture.

Making small talk in any situation can be a challenge, but when you attempt to connect across cultures, choosing the wrong topic can lead to disaster. Here are some guidelines:

Avoid:

✗ Controversial events in their home country.

✗ Excessive sports talk.

✗ Discussing pets. (Other cultures view animals differently.)

✗ Telling sexist, racist or off-color jokes, or sarcastic humor. (This is true in North America too!)

Do:

✔ Discuss places of local interest, such as restaurants.

✔ Ask about national holidays or celebrations.

✔ Ask about the marketing of medical products in their country.

✔ Talk about education in general, or their children's education.

✔ Discuss investment opportunities and the stock market.

64. What to do when agendas and timetables are out of synch

Marla, Vice President of Sales and Marketing, invites visiting colleagues from South America to her home for dinner. The group arrives an hour late, and Marla is fuming. Her dinner is overcooked, and she considers them rude. Her guests are oblivious to her feelings.

Our behavior, habits, and even concepts of time may be totally different from those of other cultures, and we are often left in bewilderment about why people act the way they do.

Time organization is cultural. North Americans and Europeans rely on timetables and agendas. Promptness is considered a virtue, and lateness a sign of inconsideration.

In cultures from Mexico, Turkey, Greece, the Middle East and the Philippines, time is relaxed and deadlines are more likely to be "targets." Interruptions are routine, and appointments may be broken and rearranged. People may arrive late for a meeting because they lingered at a previous meeting, and didn't want to offend anyone by hurrying away. What is considered rude in one culture is normal, and even polite behavior in another.

65. Understanding signals that show respect

Marco, a director of marketing, is attending a large CME event. When introduced to Dr. Wei, he gives her a firm handshake and makes direct eye contact. Dr. Wei's handshake is weak, and she makes minimal eye contact. What is considered good business behavior in North America may seem aggressive to other cultures, where modesty is highly valued.

Direct eye contact is perceived to be impolite in many cultures, where people show respect by looking away. You can show respect to Asians by looking at the desk in front of them, or glancing at them briefly from time to time. Prolonged eye contact is considered inappropriate by Hispanics as well, because it is perceived as staring. Hispanics may frequently look away to show politeness.

In North America, a firm handshake shows confidence and character. Handshakes around the world can range from delicate to firm, and from a quick, brief shake to extended, vigorous pumping. A weak handshake doesn't necessarily signal a lack of character. It may be cultural. Match the strength and length of your handshake to the person you are meeting.

Body space and physical contact vary as well. Chinese people may stand farther away than we are used to. Hispanics may stand closer. Remain flexible and adapt to the situation.

66. Shakes, hugs, kisses and close encounters of many kinds

At the end of a sales meeting, two colleagues from Quebec kiss on both cheeks. Co-workers from other parts of the country shake hands. And a Latin American sales representative gives his colleagues an "abrazo" – a full embrace with pats on the back.

In our cosmopolitan society we encounter many cultures and behaviors. For example, in some cultures, men do not shake hands with women. When Vicky, a sales representative, called on an Orthodox Jewish physician, she extended her hand. He told her he didn't shake hands with women. She was taken aback because she didn't realize the religious basis for his behavior.

Here are some guidelines for dealing with close encounters or situations you may not expect.

• Never make anyone feel awkward for not shaking hands with you. If you extend your hand and the movement isn't reciprocated, drop your hand quickly and give a slight nod to acknowledge the introduction.

• In formal cultures people feel uncomfortable with physical embraces. Other cultures consider you standoffish and cold when you act formally. Be open to different greeting customs. If you receive an unexpected hug or kiss, consider the expression, "When in Rome, do as the Romans do."

connection capsule

Respect the cultural differences of foreign-born customers.

Learn to say "hello" and "thank you" in the language of your customer. You will be amazed at how much they appreciate the time you took to learn a little about their language and culture.

– Nancy Smith Meloche
American Library in Paris

Building relationships based on credibility with healthcare professionals is the only way to sustain long-term call activity with key doctors. Understanding the unique culture, educational and social background for each foreign born physician, will allow pharmaceutical representatives to excel at selling pharmaceutical products to this rapidly growing segment of physicians.

– Kimberly A. Farrell, President
Unlimited Performance Training, Inc.

Bow or shake hands? Foreign-born physicians speak different native languages, have a variety of cultural attitudes, and various historical backgrounds. They process information in unique ways, and arrive at decisions based on many factors. To sell effectively, we must acknowledge these multicultural differences.

– Francisco Rozo MD, Director
Global Marketing Training, Novartis Oncology

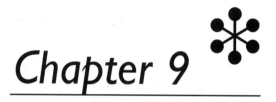

Chapter 9

PROFESSIONAL IMAGE

Managing the impressions you make

You always make some kind of statement, powerful or inept, with the way you dress.

– Robert Pante

67. Why first impressions are lasting impressions

You've heard it said that we only have one chance to make a first impression. In our fast-paced world, and particularly in the pharmaceutical industry, first impressions are crucial.

In the past when people lived in smaller communities, we knew the people we worked with. Today we expect to do business with strangers. Without the luxury of time to learn about people's characters, we make buying decisions based on quick evaluations. We have an immediate emotional response, and we act on it.

Within seconds of meeting someone we go into five-sense overdrive, registering all the new sensations we receive. Our brains automatically sort the data into categories that we've developed over time. These categories include our biases, prejudices, and past experiences. Without these categories, we'd be paralyzed by the volume and intensity of information we receive.

Negative impressions are difficult to overcome because we seek to validate our decisions. We don't like to be wrong, and once we've made a decision, we don't have time to reevaluate it. Dressing and conducting yourself professionally helps you create a positive first - and lasting - impression on others.

68. What happens during a first impression

You represent your company and your product. Every person, product, place and business has an image. Marketing departments spend a great deal of time and money positioning and developing the right image for each product. You have an image as well.

When people meet you, they do a visual appraisal of your looks and appearance to form an impression. They scan your face and eyes first, then move to your body, where they do a visual intake of your posture, body language, and manner of dress. Then they tune in to your vocal quality, and finally they listen to what you're saying.

UCLA psychologist Albert Mehrabian conducted experiments that revealed how people perceive each other. He found that first impressions are based on the following criteria: 7 percent words, 38 percent voice, and 55 percent visual.

Your visual image – what people see - is the most important aspect of your first impression, and helps your client establish an emotional connection with you and your products.

69. How to dress for credibility

Think of the power of a business suit. We are conditioned to assume that a person wearing a dark suit is a competent professional. When you are presenting before a group or meeting clients in a formal setting, a matched suit projects the image of power and authority.

To project confidence and authority, wear a dark suit with a white or ecru shirt. The greater the contrast of colors, the more powerful you will appear. Formal garments also have smooth, plain fabrics such as tightly woven fine wools. Complete your formal look with high quality but minimal jewelry and accessories.

To appear more friendly and approachable but still look professional, pair the same suit with a medium tone shirt or blouse. You can also switch to a lighter-toned suit, such as gray or taupe. Combining a jacket with pants or a skirt of a different color also dresses down the look. For a man, a blue blazer with gray, camel or tan slacks is less formal but scores nearly as high on the credibility scale. For a woman, a jacket or pants suit in a medium tone scores well.

In sales, professionalism and approachability are both essential. Blue is always a good choice for a jacket or suit, since it projects a classic image.

70. What your image says about you

People feel comfortable working with someone who looks the way they expect them to look. Managing your impression is about looking the part. In most cases, if you look the part, you will be more successful.

The doctor's white coat sends a clear message. Your professional dress inspires confidence in you as well. How do you find the right image for you? Although you have to comply with your company's dress code, it's also important to dress to make your customers feel comfortable with you.

Pierre is a senior hospital representative. His company policy is conservative, and Pierre always wears a suit and tie to meetings with his hospital-based clients. One particularly hot, humid day, Pierre decided to take off his tie and unbutton his collar. His clients congratulated him on finally loosening up.

In the pharmaceutical industry, dressing conservatively sends the image that you are professional. This doesn't mean that wearing a suit is always the most appropriate choice. Observe how your company VPs dress, and how your customers dress, and develop your personal style within that framework. You'll look the part, and project the right image.

71. Why paying attention to the details inspires confidence

Attention to detail is critical in the medical profession. If a physician makes a mistake in dosage or prescribes the wrong medication, a patient's life may be in danger. When a physician is counting on you to supply vital information, an error on your part may be critical as well.

Imagine meeting with an influential cardiologist to discuss a new medical technology that could change the life of her cardiac patients. What would be her impression if the clinical research you present looks dog-eared, your briefcase is worn and shabby, and your shirt has a button missing? This physician would subconsciously conclude that if you don't pay attention to the details of your appearance, why should your product or company reflect any greater care?

 We may not appreciate the extent to which people form impressions and make judgments on how we appear, but the fact is that people associate our physical appearance with our personality and character. Your image is based on the sum of the details of your appearance, from your body language to your cleanliness. Paying attention to the details inspires confidence. It shows that you are a professional who cares about your work.

72. How to project an image that will advance your career

Diane, a product manager with a large pharmaceutical company, has a polished and professional image. Her clients and colleagues feel comfortable working with her, and she has built solid, ongoing relationships within her company, with agency staff and with physicians. However, when she began her career as a sales representative, Diane did not project this image.

After a few months on the job, Diane's district manager took her aside to say that Diane's very short skirts and tight blouses were not projecting the right image for her to advance in her career. Diane was initially a little put off that she couldn't dress as she liked, but she realized that the image she was projecting was probably not in her long-term best interest.

Diane's competence and ability to work well with others were instrumental in her promotion to product management, but Diane is also convinced that her willingness to act on her manager's advice contributed to her success.

The better you understand the expectations of your company, your manager, and your customers, the easier it is to adapt to the situation. You'll remove barriers that create tension and your relationships will be more productive and fruitful.

73. Dressing for success in business casual clothes

Russ is an associate product manager. One day his manager invites Russ to join her in a meeting with key opinion-leading physicians, to discuss the launch of their new product. The company's policy is to wear a suit when meeting with customers. Since office attire is business casual, Russ seldom wears a jacket to work. When his boss sees that Russ isn't dressed for a meeting, she decides to go alone. Now Russ keeps a jacket in the office or his car for unexpected meetings.

In today's business casual world, maintaining credibility is challenging. The tendency is to wear what's comfortable, but this can be a downward slope to sloppy.

Don't assume that anything goes. Business casual really means dressing one level below what you would normally wear for business.

It takes planning to look professional in business casual clothing. Pay attention to the details of your outfit. Make sure your clothing is clean and freshly pressed. Complete your outfit with quality accessories, such as a watch with a metal or leather strap, a good leather belt, and minimal, tasteful jewelry. Your shoes should be polished and in good condition. Keep a jacket or blazer handy to instantly upgrade your look and add credibility.

74. What to wear to keep the attention on your "communication center"

Your face is your communication center. Your clothing can either enhance or detract from your communication.

Jarring colors, distracting patterns, extreme hairstyles or jangling jewelry distract your listeners. They will focus on whatever is capturing their attention, instead of listening to you. Your goal is to avoid distractions, and keep the attention on your face. What detracts from your image and robs you of credibility?

- Clothing that doesn't fit the situation. Dressing too casually for a client meeting, or too formally for a team meeting.

- Clothing that doesn't fit properly, and makes you appear sloppy.

- Anything extreme, such as cutting edge hairstyles, accessories or colors. Business is still conservative.

- Poor grooming: a five-o'clock shadow, too strong perfume, stale breath or ragged fingernails all detract from a professional image.

- Too much jewelry, or anything eye-catching or noisy, such as jangling bracelets.

- Men: not wearing socks or wearing socks a different color from your shoes or pants. Socks should match or blend with your pants, and cover your ankles.

75. Developing your image to enhance credibility

It's impossible to make a neutral impression. Everything you wear reflects a decision you made. The styles, colors and accessories you choose all contribute to a non-verbal statement about who you are, and make an emotional connection with your viewer. A dark, conservative business suit sends a completely different message from a colorful shirt and casual pants. Here are some tips for choosing your clothing:

- Develop a business style that suits you. Consult with sales clerks or an image consultant if you need help.

- Invest in quality garments that you feel comfortable wearing, and that make you look good.

- Tailor your clothing to fit. Even expensive jackets look sloppy if they don't fit properly.

- Invest in quality accessories and outerwear. Your raincoat, winter coat, boots, umbrella and briefcase should be of high quality and in good condition.

- Women, don't confuse party wear with business wear. Anything see-through or revealing, or very short or tight isn't appropriate for the workplace. Beach sandals or bare legs look unprofessional with a suit, but for very hot climates, conservative sandals without nylons are okay if your skirt isn't too short.

76. Dressing for your region and climate

If you work in New York City your business image will be different than if you work in Vancouver. In small country hospitals you'll dress differently from when you work in a large tertiary care center. And if you live in humid Houston, you'll dress differently from your colleagues in windy Chicago.

There's no perfect look for everyone. Dress for your climate, clientele, and each situation. Develop an image that is professional and credible, and that reflects your personality. These are not contradictions. Looking your professional best is about being authentic. You project your unique image through your choice of styles, patterns, and colors. Two people can choose very different clothing items and still look professional.

ADV
TIP

Maintain a professional image, but keep your look up-to-date. People see your face first, so pay attention to your hairstyle and glasses. Work with a good hairstylist to tweak your look regularly. Update your glasses as well. Nothing makes you seem out of it as quickly as high school hair and glasses from another era.

You know when you feel most comfortable in your clothes, and others can see it as well. You project confidence, and don't have to worry about your image. You can turn your full attention to your business and to building relationships.

connection capsule

In business you want to be remembered for what you say,
not for what you wear.

A pharmaceutical sales representative's appearance creates
the first impression that affects how I feel about doing business
with them.

— M. Tray Dunaway, MD, FACS, CHCO

I believe that people are drawn to the healthcare field because
of their underlying desire to help others. If as an industry we
think of this and take an approach that focuses on facilitating
that goal through addressing the needs of our customers, we
will have a greater opportunity to add value and develop
collaborative partnerships in the common interests of patients.

— John Brenton
Sales & Marketing Training Manager
Amgen Canada Inc.

Chapter 10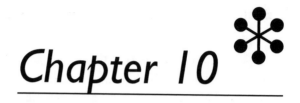

BUSINESS DINING

Putting your best fork forward

> The world was my oyster, but
> I used the wrong fork.
>
> – Oscar Wilde

77. Business dining: a meeting that includes tableware

At a business dinner with Dr. Jones, Jeff orders lobster. Wearing a bib, Jeff wrestles with the lobster claws as he concentrates on extracting his lunch. Too bad Jeff is making a better connection with the lobster than with his customer.

Dining with customers gives you a chance to connect away from the hectic atmosphere of a clinic or hospital. Use this time to focus on your customer, not on the food. When you dine with colleagues and senior management, you are building relationships too, and these can help you advance in your career.

Legend has it that Henry Ford would take potential employees to lunch. People who salted their food before tasting it would not be hired, on the theory that they didn't check the facts before acting.

At the dining table our manners are on display, and like it or not, we are judged by how we act. People who grab the breadbasket without offering anyone a roll, or shovel food into their mouths, make poor impressions. You may conclude that they are aggressive, insensitive, or immature, and question their potential for advancement.

Don't get confused about why you are at the table. At a business meal you are really at a business meeting that includes tableware. You always want to put your best fork forward.

78. How to plan the meal: choosing the restaurant

You plan your agenda before meeting with a customer. You also have to plan your business meal.

Choose the time according to your objectives and your customer's availability. Consider the restaurant carefully. Find out your guest's preferences, and offer one or two choices. For example, "I know a great seafood restaurant, and I can suggest an Italian restaurant as well. Which do you prefer?" Ask your guests if they have any dietary restrictions or other considerations.

Select a restaurant that your guest can get to easily, and where parking isn't a problem. Consider the time, and day of the week. A busy restaurant at noon on Friday may be so noisy that it's virtually impossible to have a conversation.

Cultivate a list of restaurants where the food and service are of high quality. When traveling, check out the restaurant beforehand by having dinner there the evening before, or speaking with the owner. Explain that you will be hosting an important meal, and you want to be sure everything runs smoothly.

When you don't know the restaurants in the area, choose one of the nicer restaurants in one of the better hotels. Chances are you will have very good service, and a large variety of food choices.

79. Your role as host: getting the meal off to a good start

As the host of the meal, your role is to plan ahead so everything runs smoothly. Arrive a few minutes ahead of time and wait for your guests in the entrance. If all but a few guests arrive, you can escort them to the table and let the maitre d' know that you are expecting more guests.

The guest always gets the preferred seat, which may be facing a scenic view. Give some thought to the seating arrangement. If you are two people, sitting across from each other can be considered confrontational. At a square table you may want to sit at right angles. If you are two people from your company with one guest, arrange the seating so your guest doesn't have to swivel back and forth between you.

Keep briefcases, papers, keys and cell phones off the table. Put your personal belongings in your briefcase or purse, under the table. Tuck the straps underneath so they don't trip the servers.

 Don't eat bread or anything else at the table until everyone has arrived. You show class when you maintain a pristine table until all the guests are seated.

80. How to make your ordering smooth as butter

Laura is having dinner with Dr. Smith. Dr. Smith orders a salad as an appetizer, but Laura doesn't order anything. When the salad arrives Dr. Smith hesitates because Laura isn't eating anything.

Everyone at the table should eat together and finish together. As the host, ask your guests to order first. If your guests order appetizers and main courses, do the same. If you aren't hungry, nibble on something to keep them company. If your guests order alcoholic beverages, order a drink as well – it doesn't have to be alcoholic. Point out more expensive items so your guests feel comfortable ordering anything on the menu. When you're the guest, order something medium-priced.

This is not the time to grill the server on how a dish is prepared, or reveal details about your eating habits. No one wants to know about your low-carbohydrate diet. Remember that the purpose of a business meal is to build relationships with your customers – not with your food.

When possible, order the same main course as your guest. This speeds up your service because the kitchen doesn't have to cook separate meals, and it adds a psychological boost to your guest, as if to say, "You made a great choice."

81. How to avoid sauce that doesn't match your shirt

Julie, new in the marketing department, is excited that her job offers the opportunity to try out new foods. When dining with her manager and colleagues at a chic French restaurant, Julie orders the quail hearts. Her enthusiasm evaporates when her plate arrives filled with small black balls that she finds inedible.

A business meal is not the time to experiment with new cuisine, or to struggle with challenging foods. Avoid anything difficult to eat, such as seafood with claws, ribs with sauce, or corn on the cob. Spaghetti and French onion soup are delicious, but few people look elegant with sauce spattered on their shirts, or cheese dripping down their chins. Fried chicken is difficult to spear, and cherry tomatoes virtually guarantee that you will squirt juice on your dining companion. Leave them on your plate, unless they are already cut in half.

Choose foods that are familiar, and easy to eat with a knife and fork. Most kinds of fish, meat or boneless chicken breasts are good main course choices. Most cooked vegetables are easy to cut.

You don't have to be a member of the "clean plate club." If something is difficult to eat, it's fine to leave it on your plate. Remember – you will eat again.

82. Business dining at events: who ate my roll?

It's a gala company dinner. Which fork do you use first? Which bread plate is yours?

Utensils are your roadmap to the meal. Your place setting is a square in front of you, with your glasses on the right, and your bread plate on the left. A memory trick is that "fork", "food" and "left" all have four letters; "knife", "drink" and "right" each have five letters. The spoon and fork above your plate are for dessert. Use the fork to eat your cake, and the spoon for ice cream or custard.

The utensils show the number of courses, and there is a maximum of three of any utensil at a time. Start on the outside, and work your way in.

Salad is usually served before the main course, but when wine is part of the meal, salad is served after the main course. This is because the main ingredients of salad dressing are oil and vinegar, which interfere with the subtlety of the wine. That's why a small cup of sorbet is often served to cleanse the palate between courses.

At a crowded table the place settings may be close together. Take a moment to find your setting. Then you won't drink from your boss's glass by mistake, or eat someone else's roll!

83. How to handle your knife and fork

There are two basic styles of business dining: American and Continental. American style means holding your fork in your left hand and your knife in your right hand to cut your food. You keep switching your knife and fork back and forth between cutting and eating. Always cut one bite at a time and eat it. Don't cut all the food in your plate into little pieces.

In Continental style dining, your fork remains in your left hand, both while you cut your food, and when you bring it to your mouth. The tines always remain down.

The handles of your utensils should always remain hidden in the palms of your hands. The tines of the fork, pointing down, are an extension of your left hand, and the blade of the knife is an extension of your right hand. Extend your index fingers onto the handles for strength and control. Don't wrap your hands into fists around the knife and fork handles. Don't stab or saw your food.

ADV TIP

Although both American and Continental styles are correct, some people consider Continental style more sophisticated, because it implies that the diner is well-traveled. If you want to switch styles, practice in private until you feel confident.

84. Tips for putting your best fork forward

The host signals the beginning of the meal by picking up his or her napkin. Place your napkin on your lap and use it frequently to wipe your fingers and dab your lips.

If you leave the table during the meal, put your napkin on your chair. Never put a soiled napkin on the table until the end of the meal, when you place it, gently crumpled, to the left of your plate.

Your cutlery placement sends a signal to the waiter – "I'm pausing," or "I'm done." When pausing between bites, separate your knife and fork on your plate in an inverted v-shape, with the knife and fork tips crossed at the top and the handles towards the outside. When you have finished eating, place your knife and fork parallel with the tops of the cutlery pointing towards 10 o'clock, and the handles towards 4 o'clock. The tines can face up or down. Never place cutlery that has been used, back on a clean tablecloth, or hang it off the plate like oars on a rowboat.

Speed-eating isn't an Olympic event. If you finish before others, pick up the conversation to allow them to eat. Slow eaters: it's okay to leave some food on your plate if everyone has finished.

85. How to begin the meal without leaving a "crumby" impression

At a company dinner, Bob reaches across the table for the breadbasket, puts a roll on his plate, then puts the breadbasket down. Next, he saws the roll in half, butters it, and takes a big bite. Oops. Bread and soup are the first food items at a business meal, and Bob has made a "crumby" impression on everyone at the table.

Don't reach across the table. The person closest to the basket begins by picking it up and offering it to the person on his left, then takes a roll, and passes the basket to the right. When you receive the basket don't put it down. Keep passing it. It goes from left to right, just like reading a book. Put a dab of butter on your plate and pass it in the same way

Don't cut your roll in half, butter it and chomp into it. Instead, break off one bite-sized piece at a time, butter it and put it into your mouth.

Sip your soup from the side of the spoon – silently. Don't blow on the soup to cool it. Move the spoon from the front to the back of the bowl. Rest your spoon in the soup plate, or on the saucer if there is enough room.

86. Dealing with drips, drops and dining dilemmas

At Charlie's first company banquet the server accidentally spills water on him. Charlie jumps up and yells at him. Everyone turns to see what the commotion is about, and Charlie is remembered for his "short fuse." No one likes to have food in their lap, but dining disasters do happen. Here are some tips for showing panache during trying circumstances.

- **Spilled food or drink**: mop it up with a napkin, and signal the waiter. Excuse yourself and go to the restroom to dry off, if necessary.

- **Dropped utensil or napkin:** don't disappear under the table to look for it. Ask the server to replace the lost item.

- **Olive pit or bone in your mouth**: dispose of it discretely, using a spoon or fork whenever possible.

- **Someone uses your bread plate**: don't take another person's plate because the whole table will be out of synch. Ask the server for a new plate, put your roll on your dinner plate, or forgo bread for this meal.

- **Food is cold or is too salty**: Don't make a scene about small things because you'll be remembered for your bad manners. If there's a real problem with your meal, or your guest's food, explain it to the server quietly.

87. When to turn small talk into business talk

A breakfast meeting is an energizing way to start the day with colleagues or suppliers, but may not be practical for physicians who conduct medical rounds early in the morning. The advantage of a breakfast meeting is that it takes less time and is less expensive. At a breakfast meeting you can begin discussing business as soon as the coffee arrives.

At lunch, small talk gets the meal started. Don't bring up business until after everyone has ordered because you will be constantly interrupted until then.

You can discuss business while you eat, but time your questions so you don't catch your dining partners with food in their mouths. And although you shouldn't talk with your mouth full, learn to answer with a small bit of food in your mouth. It's exasperating to converse with someone who only speaks when his mouth is completely empty.

Business dinners are more social occasions. Generally, at dinner meetings you don't talk business until after the main course, and when spouses or companions are present you may not talk business at all.

 Be sure to talk to everyone at your table – it's only common courtesy. Don't forget that your customers will go home with their spouses or companions. People who were ignored are likely to leave with a bad taste in their mouth!

38. How to end the meal on a sweet note

When coffee is served, request the bill. Mentally add up the cost ahead of time so you won't have to spend time scrutinizing the bill. Don't pull out a calculator to verify the numbers! If you find an error, quietly excuse yourself and go to the front desk so you can speak out of the earshot of your guests.

When it comes to paying the bill, the rule is that whoever issues the invitation pays for the meal. Gender is not an issue when paying the bill, so if you are female and you have taken a male physician out for lunch, if you issued the invitation, you pay the bill. If you have a problem, you can say, "ABC Pharma would really like you to be our guest."

If you expect an awkward situation, inform the maitre d' ahead of time that you are the host. Ask him to take an imprint of your credit card, and add a tip. You can return later to settle any differences. The usual tip is 15–20 percent of the bill before taxes for the server. The tip for the sommelier would be included in this amount.

After the meal ends, leave the building together. Shake hands with your guests, thank them for coming, and arrange a follow-up meeting.

connection capsule

The purpose of a business meal is to build relationships with your customers, not with your food.

Basing a business relationship on a great meal or sporting event is like building a sand castle on the beach. It will be washed away with the next tide. Building a relationship based on knowledge and service will endure the tides.

— **Bob Chester**
Professional Education Manager
Aventis

Keep face, be honest, update your knowledge, acknowledge that there are many others competing for your business. Don't fear nor trash the competition, but fear your own incompetence. Going back to the basics keeps me moving forward.

— **Francisco Rozo MD**
Director, Global Marketing Training
Novartis Oncology

Chapter 11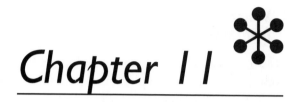

ORDERING WINE

What to choose instead of the house wine

Developing winning relationships with your customers demands more than product knowledge. Wine knowledge and etiquette are powerful social allies.

– Vic Harradine

89. What to do if you don't know a Chardonnay from a Cabernet

Imagine this scenario. You're dining with key opinion-leading physicians. One of the physicians passes the wine list over to you and says, "Why don't you choose the wine?" You open the wine menu and see: Pauillac, Beaujolais, Cabernet Sauvignon, Merlot, Sauvignon Blanc, Pinot Noir, Shiraz… What now? Choose by price? Confess that you don't know a Chardonnay from a Cabernet?

Choosing wine should be as easy as choosing food, yet for many people, it's an intimidating experience. This may be because there are more misconceptions about wine than there are antibiotics. You may have heard, "Don't drink red wine with fish," "The more expensive the wine, the better it is," or "French wines are the best in the world."

For your first few dinner events don't try to fake it or bluff your way through. Rely on the wine expert at the restaurant. With health professionals as your guests, you are likely to find one or two wine connoisseurs that can help you out.

 If you're handed the wine list unexpectedly, tip the menu towards the server or sommelier and point to the price range you're willing to pay. Ask, "Can you suggest a Chardonnay for the first course?" A sommelier is trained to "read" the guests' wine preferences, mood and budget.

90. How to select wine and stay within budget

Just as you planned the restaurant and the topic for discussion, plan ahead for wine service and selection. Don't wait until the event to find out that the restaurant you selected has wines more expensive than your business suit. If the food and wine are over your budget you need to know this beforehand so you can make adjustments. When costing out your event, be sure to include all the taxes and gratuities. These can add 25% or more to your bill.

 Choose the wine after choosing the cuisine for the evening so the wine complements the food. As a general rule, your wine cost per person should be half of the food cost. This means that if the cuisine is $50 per person you should choose wines that cost $25 per person.

By going in with a budget, a sense of the wine-to-food cost ratio, and a strategy for serving wine, you are in control.

91. Making sure your message comes across

At a recent CME program, everyone enjoyed the social part of the evening so much that the speaker and the topic were virtually ignored. When the social activity is a meal with wine, you have to plan carefully.

Although the goal is to provide a relaxed atmosphere where people can hear your message, it's preferable not to serve alcoholic beverages during the medical portion of your evening.

 Be aware that if a customer becomes intoxicated and has a car accident, your company is responsible, just as a bartender is when he serves anyone who has reached their limit. Work with the servers to keep your guests safe. Your guiding principle should always be moderation, both in price and consumption.

Check with your manager when you plan the event, and be sure to stay within corporate and regulatory guidelines.

92. How to choose wine for the appetizer

Matching food to wine implies that there is one perfect match and everything else is a mismatch. Actually, there are many possibilities for pairing wine and food, and only a small number that might not work.

Try a sparkling wine to begin your evening, with or without hors d'oeuvres. Cava, the Spanish sparkling wine, and sparkling wines from Canada or Australia, are perfect and a fraction of the price of Champagne. Plan for one four-ounce glass of welcoming wine per person.

The next wine will probably be with a sit-down appetizer. Fish and seafood are popular choices for appetizers. A white wine is a good choice for this course, since most white wines compliment seafood, and most palates enjoy white wines before red, rather than the other way around.

You can choose a country or regional wine to compliment the cuisine. For example, a nice California Chardonnay works well with Dungeness Crab, and an Italian Pinot Grigio works well with a seafood appetizer. Sauvignon Blanc from any region also compliments most seafood.

 In general, new world wines from the United States, Australia, Canada and Chile are less expensive and more flavorful, while old world wines from Italy, France, and Spain are more expensive and more subtle.

93. How to choose wine for the main course

Consider having sorbet at this point to ready palates for the main course. No wine is served with the sorbet.

Offer red and white wine with the main course. This gives guests who prefer white wine or red wine a chance to enjoy wine with their meal, and anyone who wants to try both red and white wine can do so. Have the restaurant set out two glasses for everyone and have the servers whisk away one glass if the guest prefers a single wine.

If your main dish is hearty red meat such as lamb, beef, stew, or tomato and meat-based sauces with pasta, a hearty wine will complement the food. White wine choices include Chardonnays with oak aging from France, or from any new world country. Red choices include Cabernet, Merlot and Zinfandel from the new world, along with Bordeaux (France), Barolo (Italy) and Rioja (Spain) from the old.

If your main course is lighter, such as fish, veal, chicken, or white sauce pasta dishes, choose a lighter-style wine. These include Chardonnay, Sauvignon Blanc, Pinot Grigio and Riesling without oak. Gamay, Beaujolais and lighter-styled Italian wines (usually from the north east) are good red choices.

94. How to choose wines to conclude the meal

There aren't many food combinations better than dessert and wine. One guideline is that the wine should be sweeter than the dessert. Fortunately, there are plenty of sweet wines out there. Here are a few wonderful combinations.

Port is an excellent match with anything chocolate. Port and Stilton (a blue-veined cheese) are also classic matches. A vintage port can be pricey. To keep expenses in check, choose one of these ports: Tawny, Ruby, Colheita or LBV. If there is an extensive wine list, look for a Banyuls or Maurée from France, for a match made in heaven with chocolate.

Ice wine from Canada, and Sauternes from France, are expensive, but have cachet, and marry well with a variety of desserts. If too expensive, choose a Canadian Late Harvest wine or a dessert wine from Cadillac or Monbazillac, France to gain almost the same effect. Great matches with these wines are creamy rich puddings and fruit. Crème brulée and crème caramel are naturals as well, along with poached pears and just about any apple, peach or apricot dish. These fruit dishes are better without ice cream or whipped cream when served with wine.

95. How to be a savvy host

- As the host, taste each wine before it is served. When the server pours you one ounce, swirl it in your glass and test the aroma by taking one or two good sniffs. You are checking for wine faults, the most common being corked wine. Corked wine smells like musty old books or dank gym shoes. If you detect it, ask the server to replace it with another bottle.

- After checking the aroma, take a small taste. Again, you are looking for faults. Don't send the wine back to impress your guests. If it tastes like wine, and not wine gone bad, it is probably just fine.

- You can ignore or examine the cork – it's up to you. If you wish you can smell the cork, but most smell like cork! It's more important to check if the cork is in good condition. A firm cork is in one piece, which indicates good storage conditions.

- The server should fill the glass, although the host may do this as well. Pour from each person's right, and don't fill the glass more than two-thirds full.

- Hold the wine glass correctly, which is by the stem.

96. How to work with the wine and food service staff for a smooth event

Restaurant staff and caterers are experts in the sequence, timing and service of a meal, but it's still your meeting. Here are some tips for a smooth evening.

- Provide the maitre d' or caterer with information about business meeting times and when to begin the meal service, so the food and wine service can be timed properly.

- If your guests have rounds at seven the next morning, consider adjusting the number of courses so dessert doesn't stretch to 11 p.m. Your guests may want to leave earlier.

- Advise the servers of any presentations being made during the evening, so they can avoid clearing or delivering plates at that time.

- Ask that background music be turned off during presentations.

- Request round tables to encourage discussion. It's better to have six people at a table for eight, than to have eight people crammed together at a table for six.

- Avoid large table decorations, as guests cannot talk through them or see over them.

- Set the table with as many wine glasses as possible beforehand, to save time and disruption during the meal.

97. Questions and answers about serving wine

Q. What if the restaurant has a severely limited, or exorbitant wine list?

A. Arrange to purchase wines on your own and pay the restaurant a $10 per bottle corkage fee.

Q. What if I am not confident with the wine and food combinations the restaurant suggests?

A. Visit the restaurant ahead of time to taste the wine with the cuisine suggested.

Q. What if a guest asks for an $800 Burgundy?

A. Explain that the wines have been chosen and the budget approved by your company. Or say, "I'd love to try this too, but my budget won't allow it. $___ per bottle is my upper limit."

Q. What if a guest has too much to drink?

A. Although this presents an awkward situation, work with the servers to stop serving the guest wine, and provide a taxi for the guest.

Q. What if the bill is more than was agreed upon?

A. Settle after your guests have left. If necessary, pay with a notation that there is a discrepancy, and speak with the owner the next day.

98. How to orchestrate a memorable experience

- Avoid house wines, which are often bland wines used to generate profits.
- Price seldom correlates with wine quality. You can choose local wines to keep within budget and support your region's economy.
- To make the right impression, avoid low end and imposter wines. These include anything called Champagne not from Champagne, France; Chablis, Burgundy or Bordeaux not from France; Port not from Portugal; and Sherry not from Spain.
- Request that servers give a quick description of wines to guests as they serve.

 To distinguish yourself from your competitors, provide a printed menu listing the cuisine and the wines. Add your name, contact numbers and the name of your company to ensure that your customers remember that your firm sponsored this dinner. Make sure the information on the printed menu is within regulatory and company guidelines.

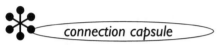

connection capsule

The goal of a business social event is to provide a relaxed atmosphere where people can get to know each other.

Your success is founded on quality long-term relationships. When you take the time to carefully plan each of your visits, you will be clearly focused on meeting your clients' needs. And when you consistently follow up on your commitments in a timely manner, your efforts will pay off. In addition to earning your clients' trust and appreciation, your credibility will serve as a solid foundation to further build your relationships in the future.

– Vicky Vilagos
Former Business Group Manager, Merck Frosst Canada
Olympic Medallist, 1992

Chapter 12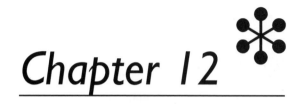

NETWORKING KNOW-HOW

How to connect with anyone

If you want to increase your bottom–line, the human connection is always the place to begin.

– Carol Thompson

99. How to build relationships at business events

Tanya and Pam are sales representatives attending their first CME event. They are nervous about introducing themselves to physicians, and spend the evening clinging together. In another corner Alex, a product manager, meets a colleague he hasn't seen for a while, and spends most of the evening chatting with him. The employees are oblivious to their guests.

Business events are golden opportunities for making new connections and building relationships. Don't squander these opportunities by talking to a buddy.

Networking isn't hit and run – meeting someone, exchanging business cards, and dashing off to the next person. It's about building sincere, honest relationships. It's an ongoing process that connects you to people in all areas of your life.

You need both internal and external networks. Networking within your company helps you work better with colleagues and managers. You'll be more likely to get the promotions you want, and have satisfaction in your career. External networks help you get new customers and partner with others.

You don't have to be a "born networker" to feel self-assured. Acquiring a few new skills and techniques can help you mix and mingle with ease. Use these techniques to build sustained relationships that benefit you and the people you meet. Nurture your network, and it will support you.

100. How to set goals for networking success

You'll be more successful at your next business event if you define your objectives beforehand. Think about what you want to accomplish, and write down your goals for the event. Here are some possibilities:

- Meet new potential clients
- Strengthen relationships with clients
- Connect with colleagues you don't see often
- Get to know people from other departments in your company
- Meet employees from other companies when you are co-marketing a product
- Build relationships with managers or superiors in your company

If possible, get a list of people who will be attending the event. This way you'll know in advance whom you want to meet.

At the event, spend a few minutes chatting with each person you meet. Then move on and talk with someone else. People understand that you aren't there to spend the evening with them, and won't be offended when you disengage after a few minutes. If you want to continue your discussion with someone, set up a meeting for a later time.

101. Be approachable to encourage contact

Welcome and encourage contact by showing that you are open to people. To invite interaction:

- Make eye contact to show you are accessible.
- Be the first to offer a warm smile.
- Use open body language to encourage others to approach you.

When you approach others, face them directly so you can maintain eye contact. Don't cover your chest with folded arms or papers, because people perceive this as closed body language. When you keep your arms down, the unconscious perception is that you are opening your heart to others.

Keep standing and moving around. If you sit down, or stand in the corner of the room, no one will see you. If you come to the event with a colleague, separate to make new contacts, and join up later. Come in with a positive attitude about meeting new people, and your interest in meeting others will show through.

 Whenever possible, eat before the event so you won't be ravenous when you arrive. It's difficult to make conversation while you juggle food and drink, and people will be less likely to approach you. If it isn't possible to eat beforehand, take a few minutes to sit down and eat, then get up and mingle.

102. How to use a USP to introduce yourself

When you meet someone new, you have 60 seconds to capture their interest. A "USP," or "unique selling proposition," works wonders. USP is an advertising term that invites interaction. When you introduce yourself by mentioning the benefits you may have for someone, they are likely to want to know more! Here are some ideas to use as a starting point. Customize them to your position, and your personality.

Sales representatives introducing themselves to a physician could say something like: "I help you do what's best for your patients by providing you with the newest clinical research," or "I organize CME events that keep you up to date on clinical best-practice guidelines."

A brand manager could say, "As the brand manager for Product Y, I work on innovate approaches that will maximize the penetration and sales of this product."

Some physicians remember the product names better than the names of the sales representatives. You may want to introduce yourself by saying, "Hello Dr. Smith, I'm Susan Jones from ABC Pharma, the makers of Product X."

You should have a variety of introductions to suit the situation. Plan your introduction ahead of time, so you don't fumble or get nervous at the last moment.

103. Introducing people to help them connect

At a business event you will often have to bring people together by introducing them to each other. Here are some ways to make this easier.

- **Introduce others based on rank**. Say the name of the person with the most authority or importance first. "Steve Jones (product manager), this is Scott Owens (new sales representative)." You give respect to people by saying their name first.

- **The customer is key**. The customer is the most important person in a business relationship. Say, "Dr. White, this is Carrie Davis, our marketing manager."

- **Help them connect.** Give people enough information to start a conversation. For example, "Dr. White, Carrie is responsible for Product X in our pain management division. Carrie, Dr. White is a neurologist at XYZ Hospital in Miami."

- **Add to the conversation.** In a more social event, if you know something about the people you are introducing, you can say, "Dr. White, I've heard you're a sailor. You might want to give Carrie some tips, as she is planning a sailing trip for this summer."

104. Business card etiquette that shows class

Tom is at a health care conference. He introduces himself to a group of people, whips out his business cards, and hands them around. Then he asks for their business cards in exchange. As he receives them he quickly deposits them in his back pocket. Within two minutes he has insulted everyone in the group.

Take a lesson from the Japanese and treat business cards with respect. When you receive someone's card, look at it and comment on it. Mention their specialty or location. Put the card carefully into a front pocket, briefcase or card case, not in your back pocket where you will sit on it. Taking time to look at people's cards shows your interest in them, and makes them feel special.

In many cultures it's considered rude to write on business cards. If you must write on a card, write on the back – never on the front – and ask for permission first.

Make sure your cards are available and in good condition. Handing out a dog-eared card with information crossed out leaves a poor impression.

 ADV TIP
To exchange cards, instead of asking, "Can I have your card?" you can ask, "What's the best way to reach you?" People will most likely offer their cards and you can offer yours.

105. Tips and tricks for remembering names

When Jan is introduced to Dr. B. she doesn't catch his name. She avoids him for the rest of the evening because she's embarrassed about it, and she's worried that she may have to introduce him to someone.

We often miss names because, when we are introduced, we are thinking about the impression we are making. We aren't focused on the other person, and we don't catch their name when they say it. These tips may help.

- **Introduce yourself clearly**. Pause between your first and last name. Chances are people will say their names more clearly as well.

- **Make sure you get it**. If you didn't catch the name, ask the person to repeat it. Say it after them to make sure you have it right.

- **Ask for help**. If the name is unusual or difficult to pronounce, ask the person to help you pronounce it correctly. They will feel flattered that you care.

- **Use visual aids.** Seeing the name on a business card or name tag makes it easier to remember. Write down the name as soon as you can.

- **Use the Rule of 3.** Use the name three times in conversation: "Nice to meet you, Dr. Smith." "What is your specialty, Dr. Smith?" and, "It's been a pleasure talking with you, Dr. Smith."

106. What to do when you remember a face but the name is erased

You meet someone you know slightly, and draw a complete blank. You remember the face, but the name is erased. Don't panic or feel badly about it. We are all overloaded with information, and meet many new people. Simply say something like, "I know we've met before, but my mind has gone blank. Please remind me of your name."

Never risk embarrassing anyone by asking, "Do you remember me?" When someone seems to be struggling with your name, quickly reintroduce yourself. They will be grateful and may give you their name in response.

If your name is unusual or difficult to pronounce, help people by spelling it or writing it down. You can smile and say, "I know it's a tough one," but don't make a big deal of it. If possible, associate your name with something, or tell them something your name rhymes with.

Establish a mindset for remembering names. When you think of all the difficult names of drugs you remember, keeping track of customers' names isn't all that difficult!

ADV TIP

Pin your name tag on your right shoulder. When you shake hands, people naturally turn slightly, and they will see your name tag easily.

107. Networking no-nos at business events

Here are some networking behaviors that make a poor impression. Don't send the message that:

- "I'd rather be talking to someone else." People who look over your shoulder are really giving you the cold shoulder. Their lack of interest is apparent.

- "I'm working the room at top speed." These people smile without really looking at you, ask questions without listening for the answers, and talk to everyone without really connecting with anyone.

- "I'm here for the free booze." The liquor is flowing, but people who take advantage of this can damage their careers. Customers and managers notice their unprofessional behavior, and they can miss out on career opportunities or sales.

- "I'm too sexy for my clothes." Party clothes are different from business clothes. Anything skin-tight, sheer or too low cut is inappropriate. Remember, this is business. Save your party clothes for your friends.

- "I'm holding up the wall." Wallflowers eat and drink with their buddies and then leave. They never make the effort to meet anyone new.

- "I'm the greatest." People who need to be the center of attention get bored when anyone else talks. They show little genuine interest in others.

108. Why you should act like a host even when you're a guest

Eva attends a pharmaceutical networking dinner once a month. When she joined the association, she found it very difficult to network. One day an event organizer asked Eva to greet newcomers and provide information about the association. Eva discovered that when she took on the role of host, she no longer felt shy, and was actually able to connect with people easily.

Many people arrive at events and expect to be treated as guests. They wait for someone to offer them food or approach them to speak. This role forces you to wait passively until someone notices you.

Taking on the role of host puts you in a different dimension. Think about how you welcome guests in your home. You make them feel comfortable by taking their coats and offering them a drink.

At a business event you can assume host behavior and do the same. Instead of thinking about how you feel, look for ways to make others feel comfortable. Take on the responsibility of making connections by greeting people warmly and introducing them to other guests. Thinking of yourself as a host – even if you aren't one - means that you won't have time to focus on any discomfort you are feeling.

connection capsule

Business events are golden opportunities for making new connections and strengthening old ones.

On making that all-important first impression, remember to stay focused on one very important concept, and that is to be authentic. Being yourself in front of a customer will make you naturally more comfortable, and in turn, confident. By being authentic the customer "gets what he sees" both short term and long term.

– Michael E. Brown
Regional Sales Manager, Women's Health Division
Berlex Canada Inc.

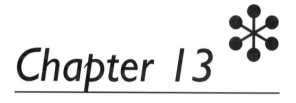

Chapter 13

SMART SMALL TALK

Building bridges
from small talk to big talk

The art of conversation lies in building on
another's observations, not in overturning them.

– Anonymous

109. Who to approach when you don't recognize anyone in the room

Jennifer, a new product manager, has been invited to a CME program. The speaker is a key opinion leader, and many physicians are attending this event. As the event draws near, Jennifer is getting increasingly anxious about meeting the speaker and the attending physicians.

If you have ever felt a bit overwhelmed in a situation like this, you are not alone. Studies show that over 40 percent of adults feel nervous about meeting new people, and 75 percent of people feel uncomfortable at business events. Here's help:

- **Approach a person standing alone** and introduce yourself with a smile and a warm handshake. Most likely you will have an eager conversation partner. In fact, you may have trouble getting away afterwards.

- **Food and drink attracts groups**. At the buffet table or in the lineup for the bar, it's easy to strike up conversations.

- **Look for a group** of three or more people that seem to be laughing and having fun.

- **Avoid two people** talking together. They may be discussing something confidential, and won't appreciate you interrupting.

110. Approaching a group and introducing yourself

To approach a group, smile as you walk over, and try to catch the eye of someone in the group. If this doesn't happen, hover just outside the group for a few minutes. Usually people will part to let you in. If you can't make eye contact with anyone, they may be engaged in serious discussion, and not welcome being approached. In that case, try another group.

Once you've made eye contact, listen for a moment to pick up on the topic of conversation. When there's a pause in the conversation, or when someone acknowledges you, say something like "I heard you talking about...," and add your own thoughts. Then introduce yourself. You can also introduce yourself right away, and say something like, "I don't know anyone at this event, so I thought I'd introduce myself."

Whatever you say in the introduction will lead the conversation. If you say, "I'm from marketing," others will likely tell you where they work. If you say, "I'm Carol Jones from Boston," they will probably say where they come from.

111. Planning better conversations before leaving home

Chances are, before heading out to a business or social event, you think about what you will wear, how you will get to the event, and even where you will park. How often do you plan what you will say once you get there? Prior to the event, plan three or four conversation topics. This will save you from a frantic search for a new topic when the conversation grinds to a halt.

- **Plan your opening remarks**. Begin with your shared experience at the event by asking about the person's relationship to the event or company.

- **Know what's happening in the pharmaceutical industry**. Read trade publications such as *Pharmaceutical Representative* or *Journal of Continuing Health Education*.

- **Know about local events**. Find out about the home team, movie releases, and books and cultural events in the news.

- **Read the local and national newspapers**. Skim the headlines and top stories for topics of interest.

- **Watch the local and national news**. You don't want to be in the dark about recent developments.

- **Look at the three main types of magazines**. News magazines, business magazines, and general interest magazines will give you plenty of conversation starters.

112. Using an opening line to start the conversation

If you've ever become tongue-tied while searching for the perfect opening line, you are now off the hook. Yes, you do need an opening line, but a brilliant opener isn't necessary. In fact, it can stop the conversation.

Think about it. When you say something weird or unexpected, people may be momentarily taken aback because they aren't sure how to respond.

The best way to start a conversation is to begin with what you have in common – the event you are attending. At a convention you can get the ball rolling by asking:

1. Have you been to (name of event) before?

2. Have you been to (this city/location) before?

3. What did you think of (Dr. Smith's speech/the keynote speaker)?

4. How do you like the event so far?

5. What's the most interesting thing you've learned so far?

Any of these questions give you an instant connection because you've had the same experience. Once you have a point of connection, listen carefully for how the person responds. This will give you important clues to his or her interests, and open up new avenues for discussion.

113. How to avoid sensitive topics that can derail the conversation

What's your goal in a conversation? If it's to convince someone of your point of view, you may win the argument but lose the relationship. Head-on challenges strengthen people's resolve to hold on to their views. After all, who wants to publicly admit they were wrong?

In a business exchange, be careful about sensitive topics. This doesn't mean you can never bring them up, but monitor people's reactions. If you hit a nerve, you may be doing damage by continuing the conversation. Here are some topics to approach gently and cautiously:

- Religion
- Politics
- Race
- Sex and gender issues
- Weight
- Age

- Inappropriate jokes
- Damaging gossip
- Too much personal information about yourself
- Your health problems or a recent operation

Keep away from topics that bring everyone down, such as grim statistics about disasters. There are lots of problems in the world, but people don't need to be reminded of them at a business event.

Sometimes it's difficult to avoid topics that stir up heated arguments. If you find yourself embroiled in an emotional discussion you can say, "Some people see it that way. Another way to look at it is…" or, "I tend to side with people who say…" Be careful not to directly criticize another person's opinion.

114. Why shining the spotlight on others can highlight you as well

There are two types of people – those who come into a room and announce, "Well, here I am!" and those who walk in and say, "Ah, there you are." Who would you rather spend time with?

Think of a time you really connected with someone new. Did this person go on and on talking about himself? Not likely. You would have thought, "What an incredible bore. He's so full of himself." On the other hand, if he asked about your job, your interests and your experiences, you probably left thinking, "What a great conversationalist!"

People who listen and focus on the other person are often considered outgoing and friendly even though they may be saying very little. Listening actively is difficult because most people are thinking of what they will say next, rather than fully concentrating on what the speaker is saying. But confident people know that they learn more by listening than by speaking. At the same time, they captivate the speaker.

Shine the spotlight on the person you're talking to. They will hardly notice if you say little about yourself. They will remember you because you made them feel special.

115. Creating bridges by picking up on topics

At a CME event Kim, a sales representative, is trying to engage Dr. Simms in conversation. The conversation is stilted, and Kim is feeling desperate. When Dr. Simms remarks in an offhand way, "My children..." Kim asks, "How old are your children, Dr. Simms?" Dr. Simms' manner seems to transform as she talks about her two young children. Clearly they are on her mind.

We get important clues when we listen carefully. Chances are if someone mentions something unrelated to your conversation, that topic is on their mind. By asking about it, you give them a chance to speak about something that concerns them. When this happens, people generally talk easily and freely. As a byproduct, they think you are a brilliant conversationalist. You make powerful connections when you show sincere warmth and interest in a topic your speaking partner brings up.

ADV TIP Although the question, "What do you do?" seems like an obvious start, it can cause problems. If you ask a guest or spouse this question, he or she may have just lost a job, or not be working at this time. A better question is: "How do you spend your time?" The person will either talk about a job, or something else of interest.

116. Avoiding irritants that halt the conversation

A conversation is like a tennis game. It takes two to play. You start the conversation and send the ball into the other court. The other person continues the conversation and sends it back to you. Without this give and take, you end up with a monologue. To avoid conversation stoppers:

- **Don't respond with a monosyllable**. When you respond to a question, flesh out your answer with details.

- **Avoid killer phrases.** Instead of remarks such as, "We already tried that. It didn't work," respond with, "Please tell me more," or "How interesting." Use verbal prompts to encourage more conversation.

- **Don't try to top every story with a better one.** Even if you have a similar story to tell, it's okay to let the other person have the spotlight.

- **Don't interrupt people**. Surveys show this is the number one irritant. Just because someone pauses doesn't mean they have finished. If people frequently say, "Please let me finish," you may be guilty of interrupting without even being aware of it.

- **Be careful about telling jokes**. What seems funny to you may easily offend someone of a different age, culture or gender.

117. Using humor and questions to create bonds

A good sense of humor draws people to you, and is a key element in building relationships. Laughter is a kind of social glue that binds people together. When people laugh with each other, tension is reduced and connections are made.

You don't have to tell jokes or wear a lampshade on your head to show you have a sense of humor. You show your warmth and wit when you can laugh at yourself, and when you observe a situation and see it from a different perspective. By appreciating the humor of others, you can be a "humor carrier" who spreads fun and cheer.

Asking the right kinds of questions also helps you connect. Use open-ended questions that invite conversation. These are questions that begin with: who, what, when, why and where. Avoid "closed" questions that can be answered with "yes/no." They make you sound like a police officer interrogating a suspect, and the conversation never takes off.

In any conversation, respond with attention and energy to what people say. Your enthusiasm will make people appreciate you as a conversationalist because they will feel you are interested in them. You will always be a welcome conversation partner.

118. Exiting the conversation with style and grace

At some point the conversation begins to wind down. If you don't know how to end the conversation gracefully, it may limp along long after you've both lost interest.

Watch for body language and signals that your conversation partner wants out. She may glance at her watch, step back slightly, or make non-committal remarks.

A good way to end the conversation is to exit after you have spoken, rather than after the other person has spoken. This way you don't appear rude by interrupting, and you don't seem to be waiting eagerly for the person to finish so you can break away.

If possible, introduce your conversation partner to someone else, so you don't leave her hanging. Once you get them talking, you can gently excuse yourself and ease out of the conversation. But you really don't need an excuse to leave. Simply say, "It's been a pleasure talking to you," shake hands and move on. There's no need for explanations. It's all right to end the conversation and move on to someone else.

Remember that you are there to build relationships. Plan to follow up afterwards.

connection capsule

Small talk connects you with people so you can build bridges that lead
to big talk.

To say that the success of the pharmaceutical industry is
founded on people is not just a platitude. Strong working
relationships between employees, customers and suppliers create
a foundation for the collaboration needed for progress.
Relationships begin one-on-one, with conduct and courtesies
that focus on respecting the other person.

– Teri Laflamme
Director, Learning and Performance
AstraZeneca Canada Inc.

Chapter 14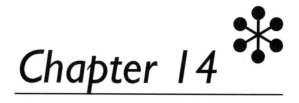

SOCIAL STYLE

Understanding and working with customers and colleagues

When two people sing in tune, it's hard to sing separately.

– English Proverb

The contents of this chapter are provided by The TRACOM Corporation.

SOCIAL STYLE is a service mark of The TRACOM Corporation. TRACOM and SOCIAL STYLE MODEL are trademarks of The TRACOM Corporation. SOCIAL STYLE material was provided by The TRACOM Corporation. Copyright 2000 by The TRACOM Corporation.

119. Understanding social styles

Robert is invited into Dr. Jones' office. He notices a golf trophy on her bookcase and asks Dr. Jones about it. Dr. Jones responds in a hurried manner and looks at her watch. When Robert calls on Dr. Smith next, he skips the small talk and gets right down to business by handing him an overview of a new clinical study. Dr. Smith interrupts Robert to say he is not interested in the study's "bottom-line," but in how the patients respond physically and emotionally to this new product.

If Robert understood SOCIAL STYLE[sm], he would have chosen the focused, bottom-line approach with Dr. Jones, and the friendly, people-oriented approach with Dr. Smith.

SOCIAL STYLE is a pattern of behaviors that people can observe and agree upon when describing someone's behavior. We form impressions and make judgments about people within seconds of meeting them. Incorrect impressions can have a negative impact on our relationships.

Instead of jumping to conclusions based on first impressions, try to be more objective and focus on people's behaviors. Observe what they say and how they say it, and the way they act. When you focus on behaviors, you can identify and implement the SOCIAL STYLE concept. This will help you sell to your customers, because you will relate to them in the way they feel comfortable.

120. The responsiveness and assertiveness axes

The TRACOM Corporation's *SOCIAL STYLE* model is made up of a vertical "Responsiveness" axis and a horizontal "Assertiveness" axis.

The responsive dimension measures how much someone controls or displays their feelings when interacting with others. When you observe controlled individuals, you'll notice that they tend to speak in a monotone, talk about tasks, and rely on facts and data when making decisions. Controlled people use their hands less, have more rigid body posture and more controlled facial expressions.

People who are more "emoting" have more inflection in their voices, talk more about people than tasks, and share stories and opinions. They use their hands freely, and have casual body posture and animated facial expressions. We often describe these people as "wearing their hearts on their sleeves."

The assertiveness dimension measures people as "asking" or "telling" when they interact with others. People who are more "ask assertive" tend to speak less often because they are the ones asking the questions, and may speak more slowly and quietly. They use their hands in a relaxed manor, lean back when speaking, and use more indirect eye contact. People on the "tell assertive" side of the axis speak more often, more quickly and louder. They use their hands in a more directive fashion, lean forward and use direct eye contact.

121. Understanding the SOCIAL STYLE MODEL™

The two axes intersect to form four quadrants, one style per quadrant:

Driving Style	Tell Assertive	Controlled
Expressive Style	Tell Assertive	Emoting
Amiable Style	Ask Assertive	Emoting
Analytical Style	Ask Assertive	Controlled

The first step to applying the *SOCIAL STYLE* concept is to know your own style. Once you understand how you are perceived, you can control your behavior to enhance your relationships. Then, by observing the behaviors of people you meet, you can identify their styles and modify your behavior to meet their needs.

Visualize a customer or colleague with whom you would like to have a better relationship. Identify their *SOCIAL STYLE* and use the information in this unit to develop a plan to improve your relationship with that person.

 It is important to recognize that no one is a "box." At any point, all of us demonstrate characteristics of all four styles. However, when we are experiencing tension, we are likely to revert to our comfort zone, which is our preferred style.

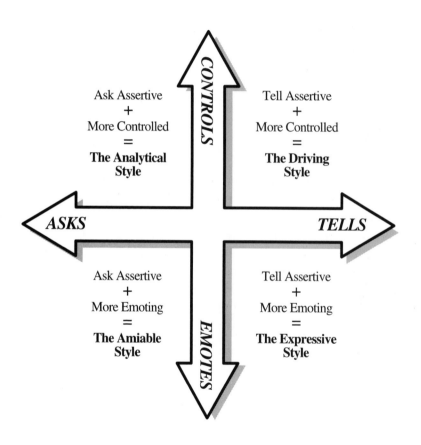

122. How to make amiable connections with the "Amiable"

Tanya describes Dr. Green, an Amiable, as friendly and easy-going. Dr. Green's nurse frequently interrupts Tanya's warm chat with Dr. Green, to gently remind him that he has patients waiting. Tanya is often out the door before she has even mentioned her products or the new information she had to offer Dr. Green.

Amiable Styles are the most "people-oriented" of the *SOCIAL STYLES*. They ask about your weekend and your thoughts and feelings. Relationships matter to Amiables, and they do everything in their power to keep the peace. Confrontation of any kind makes them uncomfortable. They work hard to build consensus, and are communicative and cooperative. They are slow to make decisions because they want to ensure that everyone is in agreement. Their biggest challenge is initiating action, especially when that action may displease people. Amiable physicians feel uncomfortable telling you they don't prescribe your products.

When dealing with Amiables, be relaxed and agreeable. Listen carefully, and use the word "we." Discuss how your products will benefit their patients, because Amiable physicians' relationships with their patients are paramount. Don't push or rush Amiables into making decisions. Take time to build the relationship

ADV TIP

With Amiable physicians you have to find a balance between socializing and business, and skillfully turn friendly exchanges into business discussions.

123. How to analyze the situation with the "Analytical"

Sam is out-going and friendly, and he finds Dr. Poole's cool, uncommunicative style a challenge. Dr. Poole is an Analytical who responds to Sam's questions about his hobbies and vacations with monosyllables. Sam has learned to capture Dr. Poole's interest with facts and data. When Sam presents a clinical paper, he sticks to the facts, provides details, and is prepared to answer all of Dr. Poole's questions.

Analytical physicians will greet you in a professional manner but will be uncomfortable with chitchat. They are fact-oriented, logical and task-focused. Analyticals aim for precision and perfection. They are slow and cautious decision-makers because they want to compare and analyze the data before making decisions. They are usually the last to prescribe a new product, but once they have decided it is safe and effective, they will continue to use it until they thoroughly analyze any contrary data.

Be systemic, organized, logical, deliberate and precise with Analyticals. Provide facts and back up your position with data. Ask open-ended questions and give them time to respond. Don't rush Analyticals into making decisions. They prefer a cooperative, slow approach.

ADV TIP

After you ask Analytical physicians open-ended questions, count to ten silently. This gives them time to think, so they won't feel rushed or pressured to respond.

124. Putting the "Driving Style" in the driver's seat

John knows that he'd better be prepared, organized, and focused when he calls on Dr. Ellis. He doesn't bother with small talk. He presents the results that can be expected, and explains how quick, easy and efficient it is to use his products. He knows that as a Driving Style, Dr. Ellis is a results-oriented, bottom-line individual.

Physicians with a Driving Style often appear abrupt, sometimes to the point of being rude. They are forceful and dynamic. They dislike wasting time, including time spent on chitchat or social niceties, and become impatient very quickly. They don't hesitate to challenge people's views.

To connect with Driving Style individuals, be business-like and factual. Provide precise, organized information. Skip the details and present an executive summary. Provide options and the facts to back them up. Then let the Driving Style individual make the decision.

Driving Style physicians are not looking for a friend, they are looking for results. Get to the point quickly. Use words like "bottom-line, "results", "efficient", and "productive". These will capture the Driving Style's attention and give them incentive to listen to what you say.

125. Express yourself with the "Expressive"

When Heidi has a new product to sell, she calls on her Expressive physicians first, because Expressive physicians tend to be early adopters. They are visionary individuals who thrive in a constantly changing, dynamic environment. People with an Expressive style are creative, enthusiastic, and engaging. They display their feelings and emotions readily, and show a flare for the dramatic.

Expressives are "I" focused and thrive on personal approval. They are active and forceful, and make their presence known. They see the big picture rather than the details, and may seem disorganized. They are relationship-oriented rather than task-focused. Expressives need to feel appreciated and accepted, and dislike being isolated or ignored.

When working with Expressives, turn the spotlight on them. Share stories and show enthusiasm for their ideas. Be open and responsive, warm and approachable. When presenting your products, talk about how prescribing them will make the physicians look good in the eyes of their patients.

 Expressives are very creative and good at brainstorming. They also like to express their opinions. Ask your Expressive doctors what they think of your products, and see if they have suggestions for communicating your message in a more interesting or stimulating manner. If your Expressive physicians are well respected, ask them for testimonials about your products and for permission to quote them.

126. Alleviate tension when dealing with Driving and Analytical styles

When people's usual manners of dealing with tension don't work, they may demonstrate more extreme behaviors. This extreme form of behavior is called "Backup Behavior." Each style has its own distinctive backup behavior.

Driving Style individuals are action orientated and need results. When things aren't going as planned, they become autocratic and take charge of the situation to achieve their objectives. Their controlling, "my way or the highway" attitude can be counter-productive for building relationships.

To deal with autocratic backup behavior, be accommodating rather than competitive. Look for ways to help these individuals achieve their goals. If you disagree with their approach, be firm but cooperative in standing up for your point of view. Driving Style individuals will respect you if your ideas help them achieve results.

Analyticals need to be accurate and precise, and like to think before they act. When faced with an overly enthusiastic or pushy salesperson or colleague, Analyticals become even less communicative. Their avoidance behavior may manifest itself as asking for more information or for time to think it over.

When Analyticals are avoiding you, don't ask for more participation. Instead, give them time to think and re-focus, but set a realistic deadline for them to respond.

127. Lessen the stress when dealing with Amiables and Expressives

An Amiable's primary focus is on relationships. As a result, Amiables try to avoid conflict and will go along or acquiesce to minimize conflict.

Amiables appear to agree, but in reality they don't commit to anything. When you encounter this behavior, ask Amiables for suggestions on how to work together to make everyone feel more comfortable. Help the Amiable become involved in the decision-making process. Follow up with an easy step to take, and continue to ask for help and suggestions.

The Expressive needs personal approval, and frequently acts spontaneously. Under stress, Expressives can become angry and even verbally abusive. They may attack by venting their feelings. Their behavior is emotional and assertive, and stems from a desire to be noticed and validated.

When an Expressive is venting, be a sympathetic listener without getting drawn into the argument. Once the tirade is over, show interest in the Expressive's ideas. Brainstorm alternative ideas. Focus on the fun, unusual or creative aspects of the situation to stimulate the Expressive. They appreciate people who are enthusiastic and inspire others.

connection capsule

Tailor your approach to each customer so he or she feels comfortable working with you.

It is up to each person to use his or her talents and unique personality to develop long-lasting relationships with their clients. First, do what you love. If you wake up every morning dreading your job, you're in the wrong place. Be honest and sincere. Don't be afraid to say things as they are - good or not so good. Don't make promises you cannot keep. First, think of your clients as the people behind the positions or titles. Second, think of them as clients.

– Michel Brasseur
Sales Director
Fuji Photo Film Canada

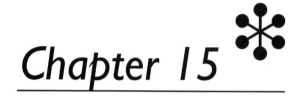

Chapter 15

MANAGING PRIORITIES

Organizing and prioritizing to maximize productivity

Nothing is so dear and precious as time.

– Rabelais

128. Why managing priorities is vital to success

There's an old Irish saying, "When God made time, he made plenty of it." We all have the same 24 hours each day, 168 hours each week and 8736 hours a year. It may be the most democratic element in our lives. So how come it doesn't feel that way? How come we often feel we are out of time? Why do some people accomplish a great deal, while others are buried in a sea of "to-do" lists?

Organizing your time is vital to reaching your personal and business goals. Nothing is more important to your success than how you manage priorities. On her deathbed, Queen Elizabeth I said, "I'll give everything I own for one more moment of time!"

Time is non-negotiable. You can't buy it or sell it, or get it from anyone. To be in control you have to manage your priorities. Managing your priorities well:

- Alleviates pressure and stress because you know what's most important
- Makes you more efficient and effective so you accomplish more
- Gives you a reputation for reliability and trustworthiness
- Enables you to focus on important tasks, and drop low-return activities
- Helps you understand that you can't do everything

129. Writing down your goals to help you reach them

In his book, *The 7 Habits of Highly Effective People*, Stephen R. Covey says, "Start with the end in mind." Planning starts with writing down your goals. Why write them down when you can just think about them? Writing down your goals gives them power. It has been proven that when you write down your goals and post them where you can see them, you are much more enthusiastic about achieving them, and are far more likely to succeed.

When you write your goals, be specific so you can measure your success. Your goals should be SMART: Specific, Measurable, Achievable, Relevant and Time-limited. Write a completion date for each activity. For example, "By October 5, twelve physicians will have agreed to attend my CME event on October 15."

Now start listing the activities that lead you towards your goal. If you work in a team, post the name of the person responsible for completing each task. For example:

Stephanie: Write and send invitations by September 9

Richard: Follow-up with physicians who have not responded, by September 16

ADV TIP

Beware of "someday." We often say, "Some day I'll…." Some day isn't a day of the week!

130. Prioritizing to reach your goals more quickly

Selena is a marketing manager. She asks the person she works with at the agency how long it will take to create a visual aid for a pending product launch. The response is, "How much time are you giving us?" Activities have a way of expanding to fill the time available. Decide how much time you can allocate to something, and you will be likely to complete it in that time.

At the conclusion of each business day, take ten minutes to plan the next one. Planning the night before gives you three benefits:

1. You'll save time because the day's events are still fresh in your mind.

2. Once your priorities for the next day are written down, you can forget about them and relax for the evening.

3. You start the next day by immediately diving into your most important tasks, without having to wonder, "Where do I start?"

Ask yourself: "What do I want to accomplish today?" Write your "to-do" list, then assign a priority to each item − A, B or C. Work on the A's first, then the B's, and finally the C's. Resist the urge to get the easiest and most enjoyable work done first. If you do, you may never get to your priorities.

131. How to achieve your peak potential

We all have peaks and valleys during the day. When your energy level is highest, don't waste time reading the paper. Use high-energy time for making your most difficult calls, writing, and preparing presentations. Use low-energy time for routine tasks such as filing and paperwork.

During peak working times, do whatever you can to eliminate interruptions. If someone drops by your office, ask if you can reschedule for later. One trick is to stand up and say, "It's too bad I can't give you my full attention right now. Can we meet at 3 p.m. instead?" Now you've even given them a benefit for rescheduling.

Tell people who call you that you would like to talk to them and ask, "When would be a better time than now?" Be sure to call back when you said you would. You will be considered gracious, and still be in control of your time.

Throughout the day ask yourself, "What's the best use of my time right now?" After lunch, identify the tasks you can least afford to put off and focus on them, even if it means altering your original schedule.

132. How to dig out from the deluge of papers

Matt is "organizationally challenged". His papers are scattered all over his desk, and he often wastes precious time searching for elusive slips of paper. One day a colleague offers to help Matt get organized. She piles all the paper in a box and leaves it beside his desk. A month later she asks Matt if he has opened the box. To his surprise, he hasn't.

 Much of the paper we keep is not important. Here are some management tips:

- File papers by asking, "Where would I look for this?" rather than, "Where should I put this?"

- Touch each paper only once and make a decision about it. To sensitize yourself, tear off a corner of the paper each time you look at it or touch it. When the paper is almost in shreds, you'll realize how many times you looked at it without taking action.

- Use a "bring-forward" file, dated 1 to 31. Put a request from your district sales manager for information about your key physicians, needed for November 25, in the slot for November 24. Book time in your planner to work on that request beforehand.

- Write "Discard by" on the top of papers you need for a limited time. Get rid of them when the date has passed.

133. How to use your time planner effectively

When you put items in your planner, do you record projects or appointments but forget to block time to do the task associated with these items? For example, if the next product launch takes place in three months, you need to record the actual launch meeting as well as block time for all the work associated with that launch.

In your planner, record contact information for your manager and colleagues. Whenever you think of information you need to give someone, or questions that need to be addressed, record them as well.

Keep all the details related to an event or customer in the same place for easy reference. When you visit a clinic in your territory, you'll have the information you need at your fingertips. Include personal information as well, so you'll be reminded to give your best wishes to a receptionist who got engaged, or ask about a physician's recent vacation.

It's crucial to have a "to-do" list, either on your electronic organizer or on paper. If your system is a three-ring binder, you can move this list to the next day if you have a task you didn't complete the day before. This saves you from having to re-write the list.

Eliminate pieces of paper. Record the information in your planner immediately.

134. Getting the most from your electronic organizer

- Record all details about an event in the Details or Note space in your calendar. Record the room number, floor, building, driving instructions, and even the meeting agenda.

- If your device has an infrared port, you may be able to communicate wirelessly with other business people who have handheld computers, provided you have a common platform or conduit. An effective way to exchange business cards is to beam your card to your new acquaintance. It's a good idea to have your own contact information up to date.

- Use your handheld computer to write a thank-you note, or follow-up e-mail right after you meet someone. If your device has wireless capability, you can send the e-mail immediately. If not, send the e-mail the next day when you synchronize your device with your desktop.

- Imagine how impressed people will be the next time you meet, if you remember their names, specialties, spouse's names, and where they play golf or ski! When you meet an important contact, record the following:

  - Name
  - Specialty or business
  - Physical description
  - Common acquaintances
  - Details of your conversation
  - Things you have in common,
  - Details of the event where you met

135. Tips for investing your time wisely

Establish a time limit for face-to-face meetings: List the topics to be covered, prioritize them and have a time frame for each one. You're more likely to have the person's full attention, because they'll set aside that time, and won't be thinking of other work that is waiting.

Expect the unexpected: If you need an hour to do paperwork, factor in 20 percent more time for interruptions and delays. Add a cushion of time to give yourself breathing space for urgent phone calls or traffic jams on the way to appointments. You'll feel less stressed.

Use drive time productively: Listen and learn on the road. Buy tapes or CDs to learn new skills, or record information about new products and listen to them while you drive. Keep a tape recorder in your car to capture ideas that come to you when you're on the road.

Be prepared: Check your car carefully the night before a business trip. Do you have enough gas? Windshield washer fluid? Have you checked your samples? Have a clean car at all times. You never know when an opportunity will present itself for you to pick up a client or a senior manager.

Take advantage of delays: Always carry extra reading material with you to use waiting time productively.

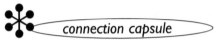

connection capsule

Managing your priorities is vital to reaching your goals.

Always respect your commitments. People will be interested
in dealing with us if they know that not only we are
committed, but we also respect our commitments. So many
representatives don't do that. They promise to come back the
next day with a clinical paper and instead they come back one
week later. They book an appointment and they don't show up.
Building relationships takes time. In some cases it takes weeks,
months or even years. But in the end you'll see results.

> – Denis Campeau
> **District Sales Manager**
> **Abbott Laboratories Ltd.**

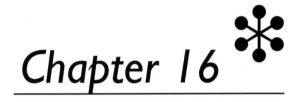

Chapter 16

MASTERING MEETINGS

Making your time count

> Those who are unable to learn from past
> meetings are condemned to repeat them.
>
> – Anonymous

136. How to make your meeting time count

It's a typical 9 a.m. department meeting. At 9:10 people are straggling in with cups of coffee, chatting about a TV show. Some people are reading the agenda. During the meeting, one person brings up an irrelevant point, and several people debate it for 15 minutes, while others silently doodle on their papers. The meeting goes overtime, and some people have to leave. Another meeting is scheduled for the next day because a key topic hasn't been covered. Does this sound familiar?

Statistics show that we spend 35 to 50 percent of the work week in meetings. In fact, about a year of the average worker's life is spent in meetings. Shouldn't we make them count?

For meetings to be effective, everyone has a part to play. The people organizing the meeting should have a clear reason for calling the meeting, and they should know what they want to accomplish. The people attending the meeting have to understand its purpose and be ready to participate in achieving the objectives.

137. How to be a productive participant in a meeting

Everyone who attends a meeting should participate and contribute in a positive way. Here are some tips for productive participation.

- Review the agenda in advance. If one isn't sent, ask for it.

- If a topic that you feel is important has been omitted, ask the meeting leader to add it to the agenda. You may have to explain why it is important to include this item.

- Arrive on time, and plan to be available for the scheduled time. Assume the meeting will go overtime by 15 minutes. Don't plan back-to-back meetings because that will add to your stress.

- Bring reference materials you want to refer to or discuss.

- Listen and be open to ideas. Respect others' points of view.

- Try not to dominate the discussion.

- Don't engage in side discussions.

- Encourage quieter members to contribute their ideas.

- Turn your cell phone or pager off, or use the vibrate mode.

- Stay focused. Don't work on your computer while someone is speaking. People won't know if you're taking notes about the meeting, or planning your child's birthday party.

138. How to plan and organize a meeting

For a meeting to be a success, you have to plan it carefully. Start by clearly determining your goals. Why are you calling this meeting? What will you and the participants gain from it? What topics will be reviewed from the last meeting? What new topics will be covered?

Now you can set SMART objectives that will accomplish your goals. Think about how the meeting will meet the participants' needs. If their needs are met, this will lead to better buy-in and commitment after the meeting.

Draw up an agenda that outlines the topics to be covered, and prioritize them. Add a time allotment for each item. If you've ever suddenly realized that you have three hours of material to cover and only one hour of meeting time left, you know how important the timing is. Poor use of time reflects badly on you as the meeting leader.

Use your agenda as a guideline, not something carved in stone. Be prepared to adjust the timing if some topics take more or less time than you planned.

Resist the urge to cover all the little things first. These small items tend to take longer than you anticipate. Deal with the important items first, when everyone is fresh.

139. How to plan a meeting with guest presenters

Mike, an experienced representative, invites the Director of Pharmacy from one of his teaching hospitals to present to the representatives in his region, on how they can gain hospital formulary approval for the company's products. Mike plans the meeting carefully to ensure he isn't taken by surprise by anything the pharmacist might say to his peers.

Like Mike, when you are in charge of inviting guest speakers such as external suppliers, physicians or agency people to your meetings, you have a crucial role to play. You have to make sure that your guest presenters contribute to the overall success of the meeting.

ADV
TIP

As the meeting leader, it is your job to know when to intervene, when to remain silent and when to act as a referee. That means you must watch the action. You control which activities happen, keep your finger on the pulse and know when to move ahead or when to wrap things up. Your goal should be to make certain that the meeting is a good use of everyone's time, including your own.

140. How to get positive results when you work with guest speakers

Here are some tips to ensure your guest speakers contribute positively to your meeting:

- Meet with the presenters ahead of time to go over your objectives for the meeting.

- Provide the speakers with details about the audience. Discuss the number of people attending, their level of knowledge about the topic, and possible challenges or questions the audience might raise.

- Go over with the speakers the content they plan to cover and how they will cover it. Encourage them to be as interactive as possible.

- Go over the logistics, including the starting and ending time of their presentation, the meeting location, audiovisual needs, and any signals you'll use to indicate when they should wrap up their presentation.

- Ask for the presenters' resumes or abbreviated CVs in advance so you can prepare an appropriate introduction.

- Set a date to "touch base" with the speakers to review their presentation again before the meeting.

141. How to keep participants from derailing your meeting

Have you encountered the rambler who goes off topic, the overbearing participant who tries to hijack the meeting, or the silent type who refuses to contribute? Here's how to keep participants from derailing your meeting.

Argumentative participants: When someone strongly disagrees, maintain eye contact. Restate their "loaded" question by breaking it down into manageable pieces. Acknowledge the value of their point of view and ask others for their opinion.

Monopolizers: If someone tries to take over the meeting, reduce your eye contact. Thank them for their contribution, and ask others for their input.

Private conversations: Stop talking. When the talkers hear their own voices rather than yours, glance at them quickly, then continue to speak, making eye contact with the other participants.

Ramblers: Listen carefully for something that relates to your topic, then bridge back by gently interrupting and returning to the topic.

Silent types: Increase eye contact to draw them in. Give positive reinforcement when they participate. For people intimidated by large groups, give them time to share their ideas first with a partner or in a small group.

142. Structure your discussion to build consensus

Joan is leading her department planning meeting. She dreads this task, because when there's a lack of structure, she knows the discussion often goes around in circles. To build consensus, everyone should clearly understand the situation, and work together to develop solutions. Here are some techniques Joan could use to structure her discussions.

Anonymous brainstorming: With this technique, people write down their ideas. These are collected and redistributed to other group members, who build on them. Because it's anonymous, people feel free to express themselves. This works well when the topic is sensitive, or if people are reluctant to speak in front of others.

Force-field analysis: This method highlights both the positive and negative aspects of a situation, and the obstacles people are facing. Groups make more effective decisions when they understand clearly the two opposing forces in a situation.

Gap analysis: Use this method to explore the gap between where you are and where you want to go. It's a planning tool that forces a realistic look at your present situation and helps identify what you need to do to reach your goal.

Troubleshooting: This identifies potential problems and creates plans to overcome them. It helps the group make sure its action plans are realistic and well thought out.

143. How to make decisions that people buy into

Making decisions is the final step in a meeting. Here are some techniques that work.

- **Multi-voting:** When the group has a long set of options to consider, rank order the options by taking one or more votes, based on a set of criteria. This will help set priorities so you can find the best course of action.

- **Majority voting:** Group members share ideas on the issues, and identify clear choices. Then people choose the option they favor, using a show of hands or a secret ballot.

- **Compromise:** When members are strongly polarized, and neither side is willing to accept the other side's solutions, you may need to create a middle position that everyone can live with, by incorporating ideas from both sides.

- **Solitary decision maker:** Not every decision needs to be made by the whole group. A one-person decision is often a faster and more efficient way to get resolution, especially when it is based on a group discussion.

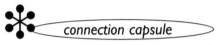

Make your meetings meaningful and productive.

Developing relationships with different groups leads to unexpected connections and opportunities to interact. The conversations that result can lead to innovations and even breakthrough ideas.

— Cathy Good, Manager
Professional Education
AstraZeneca Canada Inc.

Blessed are the flexible, for they shall not be bent out of shape.

— Michael McGriff, M.D.

Chapter 17

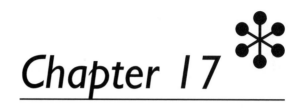

DYNAMIC PRESENTATIONS

"Guaranteed not to induce drowsiness"

I hear and I forget; I see and I
remember; I do and I understand.

— Confucius

144. Connect with your audience and create rapport

What's the difference between a speaker who captures your attention, and a speaker who puts you to sleep? Part of the answer is platform skills. A memorable speaker knows how to connect with the audience and keep them engaged.

Eye contact enhances trust, both in the office and on the platform. To create rapport, look at individuals in the audience for 2-3 seconds, as if you were having a one-on-one conversation. Smile with your eyes, and your audience will smile back.

At CME events or sales meetings, it's not uncommon for presenters to jingle coins in their pockets or unconsciously play with a watch or ring. Your posture, movements and gestures speak louder than your words, and nervous activities distract your audience. Remove everything from your pockets, and keep your hands by your sides when you're not using them to make a point. Use purposeful movements, such as counting off points on your fingers, for emphasis. Keep your shoulders back and your head up so you look self-assured.

Speak with confidence. Don't drone on in a monotone, or you'll lull your audience to sleep. Vary your pitch, volume and rate of speech. Pause occasionally for emphasis, to allow your message to sink in.

145. Use visual tools to emphasize key points

Presentations that flash, pop and sizzle can capture your audience's attention, but you don't want your audience so enraptured by the technology that they miss your message.

Visual tools focus your audience's attention and reinforce your message. They stimulate interest by illustrating points, and help your audience remember what they learn. They also take the spotlight off you.

Visual tools include PowerPoint presentations, videos, flipcharts, handouts, and CD ROMs. Each tool has its advantages and disadvantages. Here are some tips for using visual tools effectively.

- Emphasize your key points with graphics. Use pictures, charts, drawings, and photographs to illustrate your point.

- Use readable typefaces. Don't CAPITALIZE words. It makes the words difficult to read.

- Put a heading on each visual.

- Use numbers, for example, "4" not "four."

- Present "need to know" information; put "nice to know" information in handouts.

- Use the 6x6 rule: six lines of information containing a maximum of six words per line. If computer generated, the minimum font size is 24 points. A font size of 30-35 points is ideal.

146. Set objectives and plan your presentation

The first step in any presentation is analyzing your audience. Begin by asking: Who are they? What do they already know about this topic? How interested are they in this topic? What's the best way to make this information relevant to this audience?

Now you can set objectives that outline the benefits your audience will get from your presentation. The objectives should be SMART and should begin with action words such as: list, analyze, choose, explain, state, or prescribe. Write your objective using the phrase, "As a result of my presentation, the audience will…," then add the action word.

Now you can plan your presentation. Begin with an attention-grabbing opening. Give your main points and supporting facts in the body of your presentation, using visuals and interactive activities. Conclude by summarizing the main points and telling the audience what you want them to do next. Use a story or anecdote to make your ending memorable.

It's best to answer questions as they come up during the presentation. If this is not possible, allow time for questions at the end.

147. How to capture your audience's attention

Grab your audience's attention by "**P**utting **A** **F**orce" (PAF) into your opening words. The most powerful openers focus on your audience's needs and interests. Keep your introduction short and focused. Memorize and practice it to minimize nervousness. To grab their attention:

- Describe an incident or use an anecdote related to your topic. Tell the story concisely and in vivid detail.

- Use a strong quote related to your topic.

- Make a provocative statement, followed by a purposeful pause.

- An unusual statistic can arouse audience interest and strengthen your presentation. Instead of simply quoting numbers, put the statistics in a context that your audience can visualize.

- Get them laughing with a funny anecdote or story, but don't attempt to break the ice with a joke. If the joke falls flat, you'll feel humiliated. If you have to poke fun at someone, it should be yourself.

- Show an interesting object or picture to create surprise and interest.

 Don't begin with "Thank you for inviting me to speak to you today." This should be said at the end of your introduction - after your attention-grabbing opening.

148. Drive home your message with key points

What is your primary aim for the presentation – to inform, to persuade, to entertain or to motivate?

 Decide on your goal for the presentation and outline your key points. For every 15 minutes of presenting time, have one key point, with three supporting ideas. Reinforce these key points with examples and stories. The biggest mistake people make is overwhelming their audience with content. Less is more.

Think about the best ways to illustrate your key points. Will you tell a story, ask them to guess a statistic, or give an example? Here are some phrases to use to make your audience sit up and listen.

- I'd like to share a story with you.
- Let me give you an example…
- By that, I mean…
- In other words…

Develop your key points carefully to drive home your message. Illustrate your key points so your audience will remember what you said.

149. How to involve your audience so they understand and remember

- **Ask for a show of hands**. Use this simple technique to engage the audience at any time during the presentation.

- **Take a vote.** Provide participants with several options and ask them to vote for the response they think is correct. Their answers will tell you how well they understand your topic.

- **Spot challenge**. Prepare open-ended questions to stimulate discussion. Address the questions to the whole group, or have participants discuss their answers in pairs.

- **Ask instead of tell**. Ask a question about information on the slide before showing it. If participants can answer it, skip the slide.

- **Visualize.** Encourage participants to visualize how your information will affect them, and how they will apply it afterwards.

- **Guess a statistic**. Ask participants to guess the percentages of some information you provide.

- **Think, pair, share**. To engage quiet participants, ask your audience to jot down answers to a question you pose. Pair them up to share their ideas, and then discuss their responses with the whole group.

150. How to ask and answer questions effectively

"Which type of patient would most benefit from this therapy?" "How do you feel about trying...?" Questions give you the opportunity to involve your audience.

Use open-ended questions to stimulate discussion. These questions ask for explanations, invite the audience to "suppose" what they would do in a specific situation, or elicit alternative ideas and solutions. Keep your questions short and clear, and focus on one topic at a time.

When you respond to questions, listen for both the content (what they are asking) and the intent (the meaning behind the words). Acknowledge the question and paraphrase it to show your understanding: "If I understand you correctly, you're asking..." Watch their body language to determine the intensity of the question, and to check for any hidden agendas.

Prepare answers ahead of time to questions you anticipate. Repeat the question to give yourself time to think, and to make sure everyone heard it. When you don't know the answer, admit it. Don't get defensive or become emotional. See if anyone in the audience can answer the question, and defer to them.

 When someone asks a question, resist the urge to look only at that person. Instead, spend 25 percent of the time looking at that person and 75 percent of the time looking at the audience to gage their level of interest and understanding.

151. Reinforce your message in your conclusion

Nadine gives a persuasive presentation to senior management about why they should allot more money to her long-range training plan. Her presentation falls flat at the end when she concludes by saying, "Well, I guess that's all I have to say…"

A punchy conclusion is just as important as a dynamic opening. Think about how often you end up humming the final song of a movie. We remember most clearly the last thing we hear. Don't squander this opportunity to bring home your main points in a memorable way. A memorable conclusion should have these four parts:

1. Signal
2. Summary reinforcing the main points
3. Call to action
4. Punch

Nadine could end dynamically by saying, "In conclusion (the signal), here are the three reasons my department should receive additional funds (summary and reinforcement). Can I count on you to give this proposal serious consideration, and to let me know your decision by next week?" (call to action)

Nadine could then enthrall her audience with a story, anecdote, famous quote, or by showing a prop that ties in with her presentation. (the punch)

Rehearse your presentation several times so you appear natural and smooth. You'll captivate your audience with your warmth and confidence.

> *connection capsule*

Connect with your audience to capture their interest. They'll be more likely to remember your message afterwards.

In the pharmaceutical industry, there are different types of relationships that you can build, such as with vendors, colleagues, and colleagues from other companies. The main one is the relationship with your customers, the physicians.

A good relationship is based on trust and professionalism. A representative that has a pleasant personality, and provides good, relevant information in a professional manner, will be very successful in this industry.

Never bash your competitor. Never give features of your product that do not exist. Tell the physician the truth when you don't know the answer to his or her question. Get back to them in a timely fashion with the correct answer. Every high-performing representative demonstrates knowledge and professionalism. These summarize the best ways to build relationships in the pharmaceutical industry.

— Julie Drewitt
Training Manager
Lundbeck Canada

Chapter 18

CONTINUING MEDICAL EDUCATION (CME) EVENTS

Maximizing your return on investment

Spectacular achievement is always
preceded by spectacular preparation.

– Robert H. Schuller

152. How to set objectives for CME events

CME or CHE events provide you with an opportunity to meet and educate several physicians about your products at the same time. Begin with a clear business plan based on carefully thought-out objectives. Here are some questions to ask yourself:

1. Why do a CME event with these doctors, at this time?

2. How will this event help me improve my sales or build customer relations?

3. Am I trying to predispose physicians to a concept or product?

4. Am I trying to change the physician's prescribing behavior, or reinforce current prescribing behavior?

5. Am I trying to expose physicians to peers using the product?

6. What are my competitors doing that might influence how and what I do with this event?

7. What is the budget for the event?

This process will help you set SMART business objectives, so you can decide what kind of event would work best: a Lunch & Learn session, dinner meeting, organized hospital rounds, journal club, or a weekend event.

Note: CME is used synonymously with CHE (Continuing Health Education),

153. Gathering information on physicians' needs and interests

How often have you asked physicians what they want to learn or do differently as a result of attending a CME event? By gathering this information from your physicians, you can prepare a program that addresses their needs. Your customers will be motivated to attend your CME event when they see the benefits of attending.

Uncovering the physicians' needs and challenges helps you select the best speaker for the program, and it helps your speaker prepare a relevant and meaningful program. If the program is already developed, it is still important to ask your audience which aspects of the program are most useful to them so the speaker emphasizes the right information.

If you can "guarantee" that a program will meet your physicians' needs, they'll be more likely to attend. Ask your physicians what they want to learn, and promise to pass this information on to the speaker so that it will be well worth the physicians' time to attend.

Prepare a speaker brief, with your key product messages and how they fit in with the audience's needs.

154. Planning CME events for maximum results

Once you have uncovered the physicians' needs, you can set learning objectives that are participant-focused and SMART. Share these objectives with the audience so they know up front what they will learn.

Teamwork and communication are essential to planning and implementing effective CME events. Beginning six to ten weeks in advance, map out a clear and detailed plan for the event, from the initial phase of selecting a topic and speaker to your follow-up after the event.

If you are working with other representatives, either from your company or in a co-marketing situation, your action plan has to show what each person will do, and the completion date for each task. This helps you avoid duplicating your efforts or forgetting critical tasks. Use regular teleconferences to facilitate your teamwork.

A great deal of time, effort and money goes into planning and implementing CME programs. Take the time afterwards to find out the audience's perception of the event. Ask them what they learned or plan to do differently as a result of attending. Evaluate your programs to ensure that they provide a return on investment, and to help you produce even better results in the future.

155. How to work with your speaker

Your goal is to help the speaker look like a star. Brief the speaker beforehand on the interests of the audience, so the talk can be tailored to meet the audience's needs.

Physicians are experts on the medical topics being discussed, but may not be experts on your products. When meeting with speakers, ensure that they are able to position your product fairly in relation to the competition. Don't expect physicians to sell your product during the presentation. It's your job to sell after your CME events. Physicians expect the CME events they attend to provide them with objective, quality information

Introduce the speaker by explaining how this topic is important to this group now, and what the audience will get out of this talk. Give the speaker's credentials and qualifications for presenting this topic. Conclude the talk by reviewing one or two relevant points. Ideally, focus on the points that relate to your program objectives.

 If you have the honorarium for the speaker, instead of presenting it privately right after the event, arrange to bring it to the physician's office a day or two later. This gives you another opportunity to meet face-to-face with a key physician. It also provides a chance to get feedback from the speaker, and to give the speaker feedback from the audience.

156. How to make your Lunch & Learn sessions food for thought

Lunch & Learn sessions are a terrific way to supplement your daily sales calls. These events are really a form of group detailing and usually revolve around presenting a clinical study, a video clip on DVD or CD-ROM, or bringing in a specialist to answer questions.

At Lunch & Learn sessions, good presentation skills are very important. When you develop your platform skills (see Chapter 17) you will be able to engage your audience, and they will be more likely to stay and listen.

Involve your audience by asking questions and getting their reactions. Alternatively, ask participants to work in pairs or small groups to discuss which patients would best respond to Product X, or how they would treat patients that present with symptoms of Disease Y.

Use visual tools to focus your audience's attention, reinforce your message, and stimulate interest and learning. PowerPoint, flipcharts, handouts and video clips are effective because they illustrate points that are hard to visualize. They also help your audience remember what you presented.

157. Why discussion starters keep your audience focused and interested

Monica shows a DVD clip to a group of physicians at a Lunch & Learn session. After the clip she asks, "So, what did you think?" An awkward moment follows when one physician's eyes drop to the table and another physician gets up to leave.

ADV
TIP

In another medical clinic, Maxine approaches this situation differently. She provides background information about prominent institutions or physicians who are featured, and tells them the length of the video. She then distributes an index card to each physician, with a specific question related to the treatment, disease or products discussed in the video. She tells the physicians she will ask for their comments on the question afterwards. For example, "What is your opinion of Dr. Brown's approach to treating Disease Y?"

Another option is to mention a controversial or interesting point prior to showing the clip, and asking the physicians to pay particular attention to that point. This allows you to get the conversation going after the video is over by asking the group for their feedback.

Preplanning these questions helps focus the physicians' attention during the video so they are less likely to leave before the video ends. This technique also generates discussion afterwards. Link the questions to your business and learning objectives to increase your audiences' knowledge and retention, and to help you achieve the results you want.

connection capsule

Use CME events to educate several physicians about your products at the same time.

Building and maintaining a business relationship with a health care professional begins with an in-depth knowledge of your products. This increases credibility and allows representatives to offer clients added value. Professionalism creates respect and, in the long term, opens doors.

– Sophie Archambault
Associate Director of Sales
Pfizer Canada

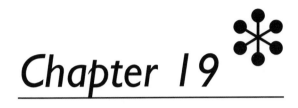

Chapter 19

EXHIBITS AND CONVENTIONS

Getting the most for your time and your dollar

> The true measure of your show's success is business. How much new business can you attribute to your show participation?
>
> – Barry Siskind

158. Planning ahead for successful exhibiting

If you've ever exhibited at a medical convention, you know the experience can be exhilarating, chaotic and exhausting. An exhibition booth gives you a unique opportunity to meet a large number of people in a short time. You can connect with potential customers and build on existing relationships.

A successful conference starts with a carefully thought out plan of action. This plan gives you direction, establishes goals and creates a yardstick to measure results. To determine your objectives, ask yourself, "Why should I exhibit? What's in it for me and my company?"

In the pharmaceutical and biotech industries there are many reasons to exhibit. You can raise awareness about your products and your company, gather market and competitive information, and gain access to customers that may be difficult to see. With creativity, you'll find other reasons for adding exhibits to your marketing plan.

Following up after a convention is critical. After the event, you can build on the relationships you began, and sell your products. Being clear on your objectives up-front helps you to organize yourself and your resources during the show and afterwards, so you can maximize results.

159. How to get visitors to come to your booth

What if you spend lots of time and money creating a great display that nobody visits? Without a pre-show promotion plan you are living the field-of-dreams syndrome - "Build it and they will come".

Industry research shows that 76 percent of attendees decide who to see and what events to attend before the event. Your promotion plan is to get on the agenda of the people you want to meet.

Formal invitation: A formal invitation to visit your booth is one of the most effective pre-show promotion tools. Try to get a list of registered attendees so you can send invitations to specific people. When possible, fax a reminder a week before the convention and then e-mail them again two to three days before the convention.

Lead card: A lead card is the most effective method for gathering and recording the key information you need from your visitors. Complete the lead card in front of visitors. If you feel uncomfortable doing this, ask their permission. Most attendees make decisions after the conference. Gathering good lead information and following up promptly will increase your results dramatically. (See page 239 for a sample lead card.)

160. How to greet visitors at your booth

Every visitor to your booth has unique needs, and deserves your undivided attention. This is fine when you have time to talk and listen, but visitors tend to arrive in clumps, usually during breaks and at lunch. Managing this rush of people can be challenging. Many pharmaceutical representatives deal with this situation by presenting a canned detail, or just by talking more quickly!

When the booth is busy, get right down to business. You can say: "Where are you located, Dr. Smith?" or, "What did you think of Dr. Green's talk?"

When the booth is quiet you want to attract visitors. To do this, try to make eye contact with people passing by. When you meet their gaze, smile warmly, and ask open-ended questions that invite interaction. Formulate these questions in advance, so you're ready. For example, "How's the conference going for you, Dr. Smith?" or "What's the most interesting session you've attended so far?

Don't ask, "How are you today?" The question is meaningless, and can be perceived as insincere. Avoid questions you aren't prepared to answer. For example, don't ask, "Have you heard about our multi-centered clinical trial?" unless you are prepared to discuss the details with your customer.

161. How to engage visitors and present information

At the booth you take your visitor through four stages: approaching, qualifying, presenting and disengaging. At each step you glean valuable information.

Pharmaceutical representatives have a unique advantage. Even on your regular sales calls you often have only a few minutes to connect with a physician. At the booth you can draw on the skills you use in short calls. Capture the physicians' attention and engage them in conversation by asking open-ended questions. Use the questions on your lead card to help you.

Now your dilemma is deciding what to tell them. You don't want your presentation to be too long, or to provide too much information. The key to an effective booth presentation is to remember that an exhibition is big, noisy and exciting. It's a place to capture a visitor's interest, but it's not the best place for a detailed discussion.

 Memorize the following mantra: "Ask and answer questions that tell customers what they want to know (what is on their mind at the moment), not what you think they need to know. Save the details for a follow-up call. It's true that doctors need comprehensive information about your products to prescribe them properly, but not now. It's too much information presented in the wrong environment.

162. How to disengage from visitors

Marlene is at her company's booth at a medical convention. She's spent some time speaking to a physician, and is enjoying the discussion. The physician is very talkative, however, and Marlene doesn't know how to wrap up the conversation without appearing impolite.

Some visitors would chat all day if they could, but when they monopolize you, they are squandering time – both yours and theirs. Disengaging is not rude or impolite - it's the logical end to a conversation. If you handle it properly, visitors will leave with a positive feeling about you, your company and your products. Try this:

1. **Change the mood:** Stop talking business and indicate that the conversation is drawing to a close. "Dr. Smith, it has been great talking with you today."

2. **Transition:** "I realize that you don't have much time before the next session starts."

3. **Give the customer something:** "Dr. Smith, here are the studies we spoke about. I'm looking forward to meeting with you next week. Enjoy the rest of the conference."

163. Generating interest in your exhibition materials

You probably left the last conference you attended carrying a bag crammed with brochures. You took the brochures because the information was interesting, you couldn't say no, and because… they were free. Back at the office you're overwhelmed by your overflowing delegate bag and put it away for a rainy day.

As an exhibitor, you bring a great deal of support material to the show. Your company pays for production, shipping and valuable booth space. Yet according to studies, 85–90 percent of this material isn't read.

Support materials tell your customers who you are and how you can help them. These materials might include surveys, questionnaires, and forms to gather information or elicit feedback on new approaches, products or promotions.

Visual aids and clinical studies piled high on a table can be an eyesore. To give your materials value, display a few copies on a rack, marked "booth copy." When attendees express interest, offer to send it. You can say, "Rather than having you carry more brochures, give me your name and address and I'll send (or bring) the materials to your office after the show."

164. Booth activities that are "Good Busy and "Bad Busy"

Your booth is empty. Suddenly a visitor crosses the invisible line into your booth, and your quiet booth becomes a people magnet. A busy booth draws traffic.

Most booths are quiet during seminars, and overwhelmed at the breaks. How do you handle this? There are activities that are good-busy and bad-busy.

Good-busy activities are pro-active. Bad-busy activities are reactive. They are the activities you use to avoid doing the things you really should do (good-busy). This includes talking to a visitor too long because you have no one else to talk to.

Here are some examples of bad booth activities: talking on your cell phone, catching up on paperwork, chatting with colleagues, fraternizing with neighbors, having your back towards the aisle, having lunch in the booth, or reading a book or magazine.

Good booth activities include engaging visitors who walk by, smiling, looking approachable, and staying focused on your reasons for being there.

Good-busy sends the message, "I'm here and waiting to help you." Bad-busy says, "I'm tired and bored and wish this darn convention was over." Now, if you were the customer, which exhibitor would you rather approach?

165. Following up for success after the convention

A follow-up strategy is vital to your convention plan. Begin by identifying and sorting your visitors into categories:

"Hot" customers require immediate follow-up, such as providing them with the clinical papers they requested. You can also call for an appointment to see if they would be interested in participating in a clinical trial or speaking at a CME event.

"Warm" customers have long-term potential and are worth contacting for an appointment after the show.

The contact you make at exhibits can extend beyond meeting with customers. Exhibits also provide the opportunity to connect with pharmaceutical industry consultants, hospital administrators, academics, association executives, the media, authors, speakers, and experts from companies who sell complementary products (for example, a medical device that enhances your product). These people can be important centers of influence who can help position your product with the customers you share.

If your company allows it, follow up by sending a personal letter, or even better, a handwritten note to thank the visitor for stopping by your booth. Attach the materials they requested.

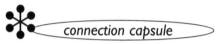

connection capsule

The key to successful exhibiting is follow up.

When you are first introduced, nothing can be better than standing tall, looking the person in the eye, offering a firm handshake and saying with a smile, "I am pleased to meet you Ms Jones!"

You gain three important things immediately: trust from your posture and eye contact, warmth from your smile and handshake, and admiration for remembering and using their name.

– Vic Harradine
Former Director, National Sales
Mead Johnson Canada

General Manager
Bristol-Myers Squibb
Australia, New Zealand

Chapter 20

TELEPHONE TACTICS

Tips to get your message across

Others don't get an impression of you. You give them
an impression. Each time you pick up the phone, you
get to decide what impression you want to leave.

– Tom Stoyan
Canada's Sales Coach

166. Why your first impression on the phone may be your only impression

When you're on the phone with a client, boss or colleague, you're playing the roles of good-will ambassador, problem solver, public relations representative, and more. Whether you're having a good day or a bad day, your telephone call is a performance that should leave your listener feeling positive about you.

There are no visual clues on the telephone. The person you are speaking to cannot see how you are dressed, your body language, or your office. The only criteria for pursuing the business relationship are the words you use, and the way you use your voice. If you sound insecure or insincere, you won't come across well.

When you call someone, be prepared to adjust to the person's tone and mood within five seconds. Listen carefully to how they speak, and take it from there.

At least 75 percent of the business we conduct begins with a phone call. In some cases it's the only contact we have with a person. Peoples' conclusions about your ability and trustworthiness are based on your voice and telephone manner. The way you sound on the telephone is the first, and sometimes the only, impression you get to make.

167. Projecting warmth and sincerity on the phone

Do people often ask you to repeat what you just said? You may be mumbling or not enunciating clearly. If people constantly interrupt you, you may be speaking too slowly, or you may be speaking so quickly they can't catch what you're saying. Listen to your voice message to monitor the pace, tone and volume. A good telephone voice is clear and loud enough for people to hear, without sounding harsh or shrill.

Energy is important to the quality of your voice. When you are sitting, your diaphragm is compressed. When you stand up and move around, you breathe more freely. You have more energy, which comes across in your voice.

 Another trick is to smile when you speak. It's almost impossible to have a negative tone when you're smiling. Although the person on the other end won't see the smile, the warmth that comes from a smile will come across the phone line. When you hear the voice of someone you know, put a little extra energy and warmth into your voice. Make the person feel really special.

168. Making your phone calls efficient and effective

- **Know the reason for your call** and prepare by jotting down key points to discuss. Putting it in writing will help you stay focused, and lower your chances of getting sidetracked, or forgetting important items.

- **Prepare the materials you need,** including a pen and paper, your calendar for setting appointments, and information from previous contacts. This way you avoid putting someone on hold while you search for facts or figures you need.

- **Stick to your point** and keep it brief. If you are friendly with the person, it's fine to ask how they've been, but monitor their voice. If they sound hurried, get to the point or ask when would be a good time to call back.

- **Take notes.** During the call, write down the relevant points you discussed. This shows your efficiency and attention to detail, and helps avoid repeat phone calls for the same information.

- **Don't do other tasks** when you're on the phone. The person you're talking to may hear you clicking on your keyboard, eating, smoking, drinking or chewing gum. They'll realize you aren't giving them your full attention.

169. Meaningful messages that move things along

How often have you received a voice message like this: "Oh, hi, I was thinking about..."? The message rambles on for five minutes without ever getting to the point. What a waste of time.

Every business phone call should have specific information that will move the conversation along. Think about what your listener needs to know or do. Does this person need to call you back, do something, or send you something? Or are you leaving information to update a previous contact? You may be able to resolve your problem without another phone call.

 At the start of your call, summarize your message. For example, "I'm calling for three reasons. I need to know the time of the meeting tomorrow, who to contact about Product X before the meeting, and which reports you need." Whenever possible, leave instructions about how and when the other person can best reach you - the more specific and concise the better.

170. Leaving messages that people will return

"Hi, it's Paul. Call me at (214) 335-3984 #42312." Did you get that? Or was it too many numbers too fast? If you have to replay Paul's message several times to catch the number, you might just skip it and go on to the next message.

Consider signaling what's coming up by saying something like, "Hi, it's Paul. I'd appreciate a call back so I'll leave you my number. It's area code 214. The number is 335-3983. My extension is 42312." Notice how a little language between the numbers makes them easier to catch.

We know our own numbers so we may not realize how quickly we rattle off a string of numerals. With area codes and extension numbers added to the list, it's difficult to get this all down. When you say your number, imagine the person writing it. Say each digit separately: "3-9-8-4" rather than "39 84," and pause after each group of numerals.

Always leave your return number, including the area code. Your listener may be on the road and not have access to their phone directory. Leaving your number is a small courtesy that saves your listener time and trouble, and is likely to get you a call back. Make it easy for people to connect with you.

171. Voice messages that won't cause hang-ups

Your voice message should be warm and welcoming, and it should let people know if they've reached a voice message. Sometimes it's difficult to tell!

- Plan and practice a message that is friendly, concise and informative. Your message doesn't have to be an encyclopedia of information. People don't need to know where you might be. They need to know if you are in the office, or out of town.

- Begin with a sincere, brief greeting. Then give concise information that helps your caller get to the next step. For example, "Hello. You've reached Karen Black's voice mail. For Tuesday, June 4, I'm in the office. Kindly leave a message, and I'll get back to you by the end of the business day," or "I'll be out of the office from the 23rd to the 25th, but I'll be checking my messages, and return your call on the 26th."

- Ideally, update your message daily, leaving today's date. This tells your callers that you check your messages, and it gives them confidence to leave a message. It also takes the pressure off you if you're unable to return calls immediately because you're away for an extended period.

- The best time to update your message is the evening before, at the close of your business day.

172. Cell phone protocol that projects class

Your cell phone is as much a part of your business uniform as your detail bag or your briefcase. It's how and when you use your cell phone that shows you have class. Here are some tips:

- Cell phones are wonderful for returning quick calls, or for being reached while you are on the road. They are not ideal for negotiations or sensitive conversations, where you can be cut off at a crucial moment. Conversations can also be compromised because of background noise or bad reception.

- Not only is using a cell phone in a car unsafe, it is difficult to have a constructive business conversation because you can't write notes or access information. Use a regular phone for important business calls.

- We usually talk on a cell phone in a louder voice than we normally use, so be careful of what you say in public.

- When you are in a meeting or with a customer, your cell phone should be turned off. The only exception is when there is a critical situation, such as a family member who is sick. If you answer your cell phone during a client meeting, you send the message that other clients are more important than they are.

173. Better beginnings and endings for phone calls

- When you leave your name on voice mail, say it clearly. Many people mumble their names, or say them too fast for the listener to catch.

- When you reach a receptionist, begin by giving your name. You'll sound more professional, and the receptionist won't have to ask who you are.

- Even if you've introduced yourself to the receptionist, say your name again when you speak to the person you're calling, so there are no mix-ups.

- Never assume that someone knows you by the sound of your voice. People are busy and distracted, and you can create embarrassment. Leave your first and last name whenever you call.

- Don't begin with "How are you today?" unless the person knows you well. You'll be dismissed as a telephone solicitor.

- Schedule telephone appointments for important calls, just as you would for office meetings.

- End the conversation by summing up the call to make sure each of you understands the next step.

- Be organized about getting and returning messages, and try to return phone calls within a day.

connection capsule

On the phone you have to establish your competence and trustworthiness through your voice.

The best way to build relationships is through active listening. Listening is the key to success. Listen to your customers and colleagues and be attentive to their needs.

A successful business relationship in the pharmaceutical industry is also based on common goals, mutual interests and most importantly, trust.

– Jean Proulx
Associate Director, Clinical Research
Lundbeck Canada Inc.

Chapter 21

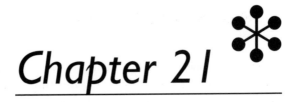

E-MAIL ESSENTIALS

Positive first impressions
the electronic way

Some people go through their e-mail like a bowl of
pistachio nuts. The difficult ones are discarded!

– Sarah Myers McGinty

174. When to send quick and spontaneous messages

Deirdre, a sales training manager, was preparing a training workshop for an upcoming cycle meeting. She sent the files to several sales and marketing people for their comments. Everyone responded positively except Ted, the product manager. He said the workshop was useless, and copied everyone on his comments. Deirdre e-mailed a colleague expressing her frustration with Ted. In her angry state, she pressed "reply to all" and everyone, including Ted, saw her heated response.

We've all heard horror stories of e-mail messages that reach the wrong people. E-mail is a form of quick and spontaneous communication that combines the casualness of speech with written communication. It's an effective tool for confirming plans or sending quick questions. It's less effective for dealing with important and sensitive topics.

Lack of context can make e-mail messages seem abrupt, rude or insensitive. When we don't get contextual clues from the person's expression or tone of voice, it's easy to misinterpret words on a page.

Clear communication is our goal in business. Before you press "send," consider whether e-mail is the best way to communicate your message.

175. Choosing the best method for corresponding

E-mail may be second nature to you, but not everyone uses it regularly. Before you use it to communicate with a customer, find out if he or she uses e-mail, or if they prefer to be contacted another way. If you e-mail someone and get no response, it may be because they don't check their e-mail frequently. You may jump to the conclusion that they don't want to be contacted by you, or that something in your message upset them.

You can tell which of your clients uses e-mail by the format of their message and the speed of their response. If they ask their receptionist to print out their e-mail, consider sending a fax or picking up the phone.

For urgent information, or when you need an immediate response, follow up your e-mail message with a phone call. A busy physician may not answer e-mail regularly, but you can get through to a receptionist by telephone to convey a message.

Don't use e-mail for highly sensitive material. E-mail can easily go astray and be forwarded to anyone and everyone. An important message warrants a phone call or a meeting.

176. How to write messages that people will read

Think of your subject line as a headline. Most people scan their inbox to decide what to open. Your subject line should be descriptive, and give people enough information to make a decision about opening your message. A subject line that says "Hi," or is left blank may cause your message to be deleted. With the proliferation of SPAM and viruses, many people won't read messages or open attachments unless they know the sender.

Avoid long, rambling messages. People don't have time to read pages of text on a screen. Send a clear, concise message of no more than one screen length. A business message should convey specific information, and your reader should know if a response is required. Use an attachment for more information, but be sure the receiver knows you and can open it.

 Use these symbols in the subject line, to move things along:

FYI (for your information): This tells your recipient they can read and delete the message. For example, "FYI: Meeting time tomorrow has been moved to 2 P.M."

FYA (for your action): This tells your recipient that a response is required. For example: "FYA: Please send the agenda for the product launch meeting by noon today."

<EOM> End of Message

177. How to avoid broadcasting the wrong messages

Business e-mail is not a conversation tool or a chat room. Respect the business relationship, and people's time constraints. Every e-mail requires work because it needs to be opened and processed.

- Send only relevant information, and ask people to do the same for you. Although broadcasting a message to many people at once may save you time, it can clog up the server and burden recipients with more information than they need. Consider the volume of e-mail your receiver is likely to receive before including them in a broadcast.

- Don't send jokes or chain letters, and if you don't like to receive them through e-mail, ask the senders to take you off their distribution list.

- Don't use the "reply to all" key if you only want to reply to the sender. Not everyone needs to receive your message of "Good point, Tina."

178. Keyboard functions for E-etiquette

- Writing in ALL CAPS or using the bold or underline key are the equivalents of shouting, and are considered rude. The exception is using all capital letters in a title of a document.

- Don't use the exclamation point to show anger and frustration.

- Don't mark something URGENT unless it is. Many SPAM messages are now marked urgent, and it is becoming overused. People will open your message when they know you, and when the subject line is clear.

- In business your words should convey your message, without smiley faces. Save "emoticons" for personal messages. :)

- Use CC (carbon copy) when everyone on the list has given permission to have their e-mail addresses broadcast. CC works well for scheduling meetings, sending agendas or providing directions to an event.

- Use BCC (blind carbon copy) to send messages to a large group, so others don't see all the addresses. Send it to yourself by putting your own address in the "to" line, and the other addresses in the BCC line. When in doubt, use BCC.

179. Why clear writing and editing are vital

In our haste to get our message across, we disregard occasional errors, and it's no big deal when we receive the odd typo. However, when grammar and punctuation are disregarded, messages can become downright confusing or impossible to interpret.

We often treat e-mail like a flow of consciousness. That's fine for the first draft, but re-read it for errors. You wouldn't send a business letter that's riddled with misspelled words, missing punctuation and incomplete sentences. Give your e-mail correspondence the same attention.

It's more difficult to proofread a message on a screen. Read important messages out loud or print them and read the hard copy. If possible, program your computer to automatically spell-check the message before it is sent. If your e-mail program doesn't have a spell-checker, you can copy the message into your word processing program to do a spell-check.

No matter how the message is delivered, it's still a written message. People notice mistakes, and while a few errors may be accepted between friends and co-workers, a sloppily written e-mail message to a customer or manager leaves a negative impression.

180. Why your e-mail is like a postcard that anyone can read

Think of e-mail as a postcard. People can read it, save it and send it to others. E-mail isn't private or temporary. Not only can any number of people receive your message, but they can also print it and use it as a legal document. Never send anything that you wouldn't want posted on the office bulletin board.

Don't send a message when you are angry or emotional. Firing off a heated tirade can cause irreparable damage. If you're upset, cool off and sleep on it, then consider your response in the morning. E-mail is easily misinterpreted, and one person's idea of a concise message is another person's idea of a rude or insensitive one.

Make sure your message is accurate, because it can be archived and become a permanent record with your name attached to it. Be extremely wary of sending anything that can be labeled racist, sexist or disparaging to others. E-mail messages have been known to reach the wrong parties.

Keep in mind that this e-mail belongs to your company. Your organization is providing the system and paying for it. Companies have regulations for what can be sent and received. For personal correspondence, consider getting another e-mail address.

181. Keeping up to date without being overwhelmed

Check your e-mail regularly to avoid pile-up. On the other hand, don't become a slave to your e-mail by checking your messages constantly and getting sidetracked.

Try to respond to messages within 24 hours if possible. If you don't have the information necessary, acknowledge that you received the message, and let them know when you will get back to them.

Not everyone uses e-mail or checks their e-mail regularly, however, and messages do go astray. Don't assume your message has been received and ignored. You may have to follow up with another e-mail or a phone call, especially to confirm a meeting.

Leave an out-of-the-office message when you are away, so people won't expect an answer right away. You can provide details about who to contact in your absence, and when you will respond.

Use a signature line. Include your name and phone number to save your reader the time of looking it up if they need to contact you. You may also want to include your job title, business address and web site.

182. Salutations and endings that are sincere and friendly

Salutations depend on the relationship you have with the receiver. For more formal messages, you can write, "Dear Dr. Smith" or "Dear Robert". If you know the person well, "Hello" or "Hi," work well with the informality of e-mail.

When you use a salutation, use a closing such as "Sincerely" or "Best regards," depending on your relationship.

If you have not corresponded with this person before, introduce yourself in your first e-mail by giving information about yourself, your company, and your reason for writing. If a mutual contact suggested you write, mention this connection and any relevant background information.

When you are sending data back and forth you don't need a salutation each time, but you should update the subject line when the focus changes. It's also polite to send a brief sign-off such as "Thank you" to end a specific correspondence.

You can use e-mail to send a word of thanks, but for real impact, it pales when compared to a hand-written note. How many e-mail messages do you receive each day compared to the number of handwritten envelopes you receive? We pay attention to handwritten notes because they are so rare. Sometimes it's worth the extra time and effort of sending a card. You'll stand out from the crowd.

183. How to send international e-mail

E-mail fits right in with our informal North American culture, but people in other countries aren't always comfortable with our casual nature. For international e-mail:

- Use formal greetings and salutations, such as "Dear" and "Sincerely."

- In a first message, address the person as Dr., Mr. or Ms. When you reply to their message, use their signature as your guide. If they use their first name you can do the same. If they sign with both their first and last name, keep a formal tone.

- Avoid abbreviations, which can be misunderstood. Write out addresses in full, such as "Post Office Box" rather than PO Box, or "Avenue" instead of Ave.

- Don't attempt humor or sarcasm in an e-mail message. It can be misinterpreted, and you may offend people without knowing it.

- Use simple, clear language. Avoid cyber-speak, such as IMHO (In My Humble Opinion) or FWIW (For What It's Worth.) Not everyone understands these acronyms.

- Avoid slang and idiomatic expressions, such as "That's in the ball park." Few people outside of North America will understand what you mean.

connection capsule

Managing technology sends the positive message that you can manage your work and your life.

To establish relationships with physicians in this very competitive industry, it is most import to be knowledgeable and credible in all your business relationships.

— Raynald Riverin
National Training and Development Manager
Bristol-Myers Squibb Canada

Afterword:

Thank you for taking the time to read *Prescription for Success*. We hope it will have a big impact on your career, and on your life. Relationship building is an ongoing process, and we would like to continue to be part of your learning and development. Feel free to contact us to let us know your needs, so we can provide information that matters to you.

Our free monthly e-mail newsletter, "Helene & Christie's Script for Success" is full of tips and techniques that give you ongoing support in building relationships that matter.

Visit www.Prescription4success to sign up.

We wish you every continued success!

Hélène, Christie & Lynda

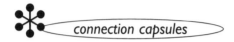
connection capsules

1. At the core of any successful business relationship is trust and respect.

2. You build credibility when your body language matches your words.

3. The sound of your voice tells people who you are, and connects you with your listener.

4. Remember the 80/20 rule: your customers should be speaking 80 percent of the time.

5. There's a direct correlation between your level of emotional intelligence and your success at work.

6. You can use conflict as a catalyst for change.

7. Customer access is based on customer relationships.

8. Respect the cultural differences of foreign-born customers.

9. In business you want to be remembered for what you say, not for what you wear.

10. The purpose of a business meal is to build relationships with your customers, not with your food.

11. The goal of a business social event is to provide a relaxed atmosphere where people can get to know each other.

12. Business events are golden opportunities for making new connections and strengthening old ones.

13. Small talk connects you with people so you can build bridges that lead to big talk.

14. Tailor your approach to each customer so he or she feels comfortable working with you.

15. Managing your priorities is vital to reaching your goals.

16. Make your meetings meaningful and productive.

17. Connect with your audience to capture their interest. They'll be more likely to remember your message afterwards.

18. Use CME events to educate several physicians about your products at the same time.

19. The key to successful exhibiting is follow-up.

20. On the phone you have to establish your competence and trustworthiness through your voice.

21. Managing technology sends the positive message that you can manage your work and your life.

About the Authors

Hélène Meloche

Hélène Meloche's dynamic presentations are guaranteed to keep you interested. She has many years of experience as a speaker and training consultant, and was Sales Training Manager for Mead Johnson Canada, and Manager of Professional Development for Bristol-Myers Squibb.

Hélène is the designer of the very effective HMC Time Management System, and is well known for her seminar entitled, *Effective Use of Your Time and Energy*. She facilitated the international management training at the World Trade Institute in New York, and presently leads seminars and conferences across Canada, the U.S., Europe and Africa. Helene's specialties include *Interactive Presentations*, and she has trained many sales representatives, physicians and other health care professionals on these skills. She also coaches speakers and trainers.

Contact Hélène at Hélène Meloche Communications: (819) 772-8463.

E-mail: time@hmeloche.com
visit: www.hmeloche.com

Christie Sterns

Christie learned the value of building relationships with both internal and external customers when she worked as a pharmaceutical sales representative, and as Manager of Sales Training for Boehringer Ingelheim Canada Ltd.

Christie is now president of Training Makes Cents Inc., a performance improvement company that specializes in the design and delivery of interactive communication and selling skills programs for pharmaceutical industry employees and their health care customers. TMC's most highly acclaimed programs include *Interactive Presentations* and *Effective Facilitation Skills*.

Hélène and Christie are strategically aligned to offer clients a variety of skill-building programs that are based on the principles of adult learning.

Contact Christie at Training Makes Cents Inc: (905) 820-0830

E-mail: tmcents@sympatico.ca
visit: www.trainingmakescents.com

Lynda Goldman

Lynda Goldman is a business etiquette consultant, publisher, and the author of 30 books, including *How to Make a Million Dollar First Impression, Business Casual or Business Casualty?* and *Who Ate My Roll?* She has appeared on Global TV and CBC, had a regular column in the Montreal Gazette, and has been featured in Reader's Digest, Sales Contact Magazine, the National Post, and many other magazines and newspapers. Lynda is a seminar leader for pharmaceutical companies, and provides workshops on first impressions, networking, business image, and business dining.

Contact Lynda at Helix Publishing: (514) 336-4339.

E-mail: Lynda@impressforsuccess.com
visit: www.ImpressforSuccess.com

Vic Harradine

Vic is a professor and director of the Algonquin College Sommelier Certificate Program. Vic is an Algonquin Sommelier (Honors) Graduate, Past President of The National Capital Sommelier Guild, member of The Society of Wine Educators, and Wine Judge at the Cellars of the World Competition, Eastern Ontario Amateur Wine Makers' Competition and Epicurean Awards. He was named 'Wine Person of the Year' by the National Capital Sommelier Guild in 1998. Vic spent eleven years in the pharmaceutical industry holding executive positions in sales, sales training and marketing for Mead Johnson Canada. He was posted internationally as President, Australia and New Zealand for Bristol-Myers Squibb.

Contact Vic at: victor.harradine@sympatico.ca

Janet MacPhee

Janet MacPhee is an Adler Certified Coach who helps both individuals and organizations optimize their performance. She has worked for a diverse range of industry sectors and has over 15 years of corporate training and development experience. Janet's passion is to connect with her clients to help them develop to their fullest potential.

Contact Janet at Compass Coaching: (905) 857-1488

E-mail: compasscoaching@rogers.com
visit: www.compasscoaching.org

Barry Siskind

Barry Siskind is an expert in exhibit marketing. He is author of *The Power of Exhibit Marketing*, *Making Contact*, and *Bumblebees Can't Fly*, as well as hundreds of industry-related articles. He is the creator of *Making Trade Shows Work* and *Working the Show From Both Sides of the Aisle*. His professional exhibit management program and training programs have brought benefits to his pharmaceutical clients. Call for a free copy of his audiotape *Double Your Trade Shows Results - Guaranteed*.

Contact Barry at International Training and Management Company: 1-800-358-6079

E-mail: Barry@siskindtraining.com
visit: www.siskindtraining.com

Diane Bussandri

Diane Bussandri is Managing Partner at Knightsbridge Bussandri Macdonald, a full service human capital management firm dedicated to helping its client organizations build healthy employment relationships. Her areas of expertise include Executive Coaching and Career Management and her clients range from entrepreneurial companies to multinational pharmaceutical organizations. With an in-depth understanding of emotional intelligence, she mixes humor and straight talk to help individuals enhance their leadership capability.

Contact Diane at Knightsbridge Bussandri Macdonald:
(514) 281-6656.

E-mail: dbussandri@knightsbridge.ca

visit: www.knightsbridge.ca

Frema Engel

Frema Engel uses her vast experience as organizational consultant, trainer, leadership coach and professional speaker to help employees break down barriers and build bridges. Her messages are simple: with goodwill and dialogue, we can easily settle misunderstandings and disputes, and forge new alliances. Author of numerous articles and three books dealing with workplace conflict and peace building, Frema's audiences describe her as a dynamic, engaging speaker who "makes you want to change, gives you the tools to make it possible, and shows you how to do it."

Contact Frema at Engel & Associés: 514-989-9298
(1-800-363-6435)

E-mail: frema@fremaengel.com
visit: www.fremaengel.com

Dr. Andy Farah

Dr Farah is the Chief of Psychiatry at High Point Regional Health Systems, and an assistant clinical faculty member at Wake Forest University. He has studied and written about medical decision-making and pharmaceutical sales for the past ten years.

Contact Dr. Farah at Farah Consulting: (336) 664-9218

E-mail: drandyfarah@yahoo.com

Other Books by the Authors

Publications by Lynda Goldman

How to Make a Million Dollar First Impression

L'art de réussir sa première impression

Business Casual or Business Casualty?

Who Ate My Roll?

10 Secrets of Successful Business Dining (audio)

To order: www.Impressforsuccess.com

Publications by Frema Engel:

Taming the Beast: Getting Violence out of the Workplace

Getting Tigers to Purr in Expert Women Who Speak … Speak Out! Volume 3

Stand Your Ground: Protect yourself from anger, aggression and abuse at work

Tenez bon : Protégez-vous de la colère, des agressions et autres formes d'abus au travail

Le stress post-traumatique et les victimes d'actes criminels

To order:www.fremaengel.com

Publications by Barry Siskind

The Power of Exhibit Marketing
Making Contact
Seminars to Build Your Business
Bumblebees Can't Fly
Making Trade Shows Work
Making Trade Shows Work: eight-cassette learning program.
The Successful Exhibitor: 28 minute video
To order: www.siskindtraining.com.

Publications by Dr. Andy Farah

The Doctor as Customer
The Ultimate Guide for Pharmaceutical Reps
To order: (336) 664-9218

Recommended reading:

Coaching

Coaching for High Performance, Third Edition by John Whitmore, Nicholas Brealey Publishing - London, UK, 2002

Communication

Communicating Clearly, Robert Heller, Dorling Kindersley, New York, NY, 2000

First Things First, Stephen r. Covey, Free Press, 1995

Power Talk, Sarah Myers McGinty, Ph.D., Warner Business Books, New York, 2002

Secrets of Face-to-Face Communication, Peter Urs Bender and Dr. Robert Tracz, Stoddart Publishing Co. Limited, Toronto, Ontario, 2001

The 7 Habits of Highly Effective People, Stephen R. Covey, A Fireside Book, Simon & Shuster, New York, Ny 1989

Emotional Intelligence

Emotional Intelligence, Daniel Goleman, Bantam Doubleday Dell Publishing Group Inc, 1995

Working with Emotional Intelligence, Daniel Goleman, Bantam Books, New York, NY 1998

Executive EQ, Robert Cooper, Perigee, New York, NY 1998

Wine

The Oxford Companion to Wine, Edited by Janice Robinson, Oxford University Press, 1994

Wine With Food, by Joanna Simon, Simon and Schuster, New York, NY, 1996

LEAD CARD

International Training &
Management Company
Tel: (519) 927–9494
Fax: (519) 927–9493

Date:_____

A uthority:_____

C apability:_____

T ime:_____

I dentity:_____

    Name:_____

    Position:_____

    Organization:_____

    Address:_____

    Telephone:_____

O bstacles:_____

N eed:_____

_____

_____

Promised Follow-Up:_____

_____

Comments:_____

_____

_____

Prescription for Success

Keynote Addresses and Workshops

Would you like to improve your skills in building relationships?

We offer both keynote addresses and interactive workshops. For your next sales meeting or training session, find out about our customized solutions that meet your needs.

Call Lynda Goldman at 1-877-462-4384

Lynda@Prescription4success.com

www.Prescription4Success.com